FLIPPING MY SCRIPT

ADRIAN ALVARADO

Sphere Media Production LLC

Some names have been changed to protect people's privacy.

Some dialogue has been recreated.

FLIPPING MY SCRIPT. Copyright 2022 by Adrian Alvarado. All rights reserved. Printed in the United States of America. No part of this book may be used or reproduced in any manner without written permission except for brief quotations embodied in critical articles and reviews.

Copyrights: 1-11775147881

FIRST EDITION

Book Cover Designed by Ewelina Lemansky
Cover & Author Photo by Diana Perez-Alvarado
Author Contact: adrianalvarado.net

Unless otherwise noted, all photographs are courtesy of the author.

Library of Congress: 2024917953

ISBN 979-8-218-36272-0
ISBN 979-8-9914523-0-4 (e-book)

SPHERE MEDIA PRODUCTIONS LLC.

DEDICATION

To my son Sebastian and daughter Natalia,

This book is for you. I wanted to leave you a little piece of your history, so that it can live and grow with you both. One of my goals in writing this book was to bring a little bit of your Grandmother Nena back to life, so you could get to know her and visualize what her love and passions were. After my experiences growing up in Jersey City and Puerto Rico, I set a few goals for myself and got to accomplish some, like marrying a devoted partner like your mother, Diana, and writing this book. But the most important goal I've achieved has been being your father. Never let go of your dreams and keep striving for your goals. No matter what life brings, always remember to enjoy the gift of life.

Love you,

Dad.

CONTENTS

CHAPTER 1	ROOTS	1
CHAPTER 2	URBAN LIFE	9
CHAPTER 3	TAXATION WITHOUT REPRESENTATION	17
CHAPTER 4	BACK TO PARADISE	25
CHAPTER 5	EL BARRIO COCO	37
CHAPTER 6	BACK TO THE FACTORIES	51
CHAPTER 7	SUCKED AWAY	63
CHAPTER 8	PARADISE LOST	71
CHAPTER 9	TYPICAL	77
CHAPTER 10	JERSEY CITY FELIX	89
CHAPTER 11	A DOLLAR IN YOUR POCKET	105
CHAPTER 12	PIZZA MAN	111
CHAPTER 13	IDENTITY	123
CHAPTER 14	HARSH TRUTHS	131
CHAPTER 15	A MOTHERS'S PAIN	139

CHAPTER 16	A BROTHER'S KEEPER	149
CHAPTER 17	CHOICES	159
CHAPTER 18	LIFE GOES ON	165
CHAPTER 19	A PIZZA WAR	169
CHAPTER 20	BOILING POINT	181
CHAPTER 21	STILL BLOWING KISSES	195
CHAPTER 22	BREAKING THROUGH	205
CHAPTER 23	MR. WONDER	215
CHAPTER 24	A LETTER FROM COCA	221
	ACKNOWLEDGEMENTS	235

FLIPPING MY SCRIPT

"La vida es un mambo; el que no la baila es un chango."

"Life is a mambo; whoever doesn't dance it, is a crybaby."

— La Coca

I was born straddling two contrasting worlds. One was a tropical island paradise brimming with love, vibrant salsa rhythms, and a sense of oppression. The other was Jersey City, NJ. during the 1980s. A city with a melting pot of immigrants chasing their dreams. It was a place of resilience, constant change, and countless opportunities to get in trouble. The overarching objective was clear: to overcome the odds and succeed.

CHAPTER 1

ROOTS

Ceiba tree, Vieques, Puerto Rico.
Photo by: Diana Perez-Alvarado

Nilda "Nena" Rivera was born in Aibonito, Puerto Rico, on November 12, 1945, to Estelle Martinez and a man whose name I can't even find on an ancestry website—a man I call Mr. Rivera. It's one of those family secrets that no one ever wants to talk about on my mom's side. There was a relationship between Mr. Rivera and my Grandmother

Estelle, but things didn't work out between them. All I know is that my maternal Grandmother, Estelle, an Afro-Latina woman, cleaned houses in the mountains of Aibonito, Puerto Rico, in the 1940s. That was one of the only jobs available to Afro-Latina women on the island at the time. Even in Puerto Rico, the hue of your skin mattered as it still does today. Many Puerto Ricans on the island were of mixed Spanish, African, and Taíno descent. The more African and Taíno heritage you had, the lower your social class was on the island.

My grandmother became pregnant with my mother when she was fifteen years old. Having kids and getting married young was common back then. After puberty, girls were no longer considered girls; they were women. There were no "teenage years." The countryside didn't have many schools for poor children to attend. You went from an adolescent to an adult in a matter of moments. Mr. Rivera, who was already married with a family, fathered my mother, adding complexity to their already challenging circumstances.

Growing up, it seemed to me that almost every male Puerto Rican on the island and in New Jersey whom I knew had multiple families. Male chauvinism was and still is rampant on the island to this day. I never met the man, but based on the history, my grandfather, Mr. Rivera, seemed to embody the historical traditions of the Spaniards and men of the Old and New Testament, including having concubines, like a true conquistador.

My grandmother eventually met her new husband,

Alberto Ortiz. Alberto didn't seem to care what anybody thought. He fell in love with my grandmother, adopted my mother, and after his service in the Korean War in 1953, they moved to downtown Jersey City, settling near Mercer and Barrow Street.

Alberto and Estelle had three more children: my Aunts Rita and Dalia, and my Uncle Isidro. They would also eventually adopt my Aunt Luisa. Everyone called my mom, La Nena (Neh-nah), which means "little girl" in Spanish. The name was given to her at her baptism. Nena made sure everyone would call her "Nena" for the rest of her life. One of the reasons the name stuck was because she never stopped sucking on her thumb, even as an adult. She always looked like a little girl with a dimple in her cheek sucking her thumb.

My mom always looked her best and had a classic look to her style. She stood at 5'6", and her big brown eyes were always painted with thin black eyeliner. It made her eyes look like they had wings. Her jet-black hair was long and silky, reaching down to her waist like Pocahontas. She had a talent for hairdressing and applying makeup and always wore intricate braids in her hair. She became a certified beautician after attending the old Ferris High School on Cole Street in Jersey City. Shortly after graduating, she met a young skinny rebel without a cause named Felix Alvarado. Felix had just been rejected from the Army in Newark, New Jersey during the Vietnam War because of his flat feet. He told me, "They put me right back on the bus and told me to go home."

ADRIAN ALVARADO

My parents met at a dance hall in Jersey City, and on their first date, Nena took Felix to eat Chinese food in Journal Square, and as they say, the rest is history. They got married, and shortly after, in 1968, my brother Eduardo Alvarado was born. My dad, Felix, was crafty with a pair of scissors and a pair of dice. He was proud of his sharp vision and later in life he would tell me stories about his eagle eye. He was excellent at cutting garments and suits and worked in a Jewish tailor shop and in garment factories in Jersey City and Manhattan.

Felix was also a gambler and hustler. Being a gambler meant experiencing plenty of wins and even more losses, though mostly losses. However, the best thing he ever did with any of his winnings was buy a piece of land in his hometown of Salinas, Puerto Rico. He built two little houses on the land; one was made of wood. It was a loft-style cabin where Nena would have her hair salon. The other house was made with the traditional local island style architecture of cinder blocks and cement. It had two bedrooms, a kitchen, and a bathroom. My parents planned to move back to Puerto Rico, but Nena got pregnant again with my brother Richard. Unfortunately, the pregnancy proved to be difficult and with many complications.

Richard was born with muscular dystrophy and many other debilitating learning and developmental disabilities. It affected my brother's life in every way, as well as my parents. I would later hear a rumor that the reason my brother was born disabled was due to my mom being given an X-ray while she was pregnant with

Richard. Everything that we take for granted like speech, sight, and movement wasn't normal for Richard. My brother needed constant care, and as he got older, it would prove to be difficult for my mom and dad to properly care for him while working full-time. Richard required twenty-four hours of nursing care and was eventually admitted to the Woodbridge Developmental Center, in Woodbridge, New Jersey. As a father now myself, and knowing what I know about my mom, she must have been devastated that she couldn't care for her son. I can imagine the sorrow she felt, thinking of him every night, wondering, and hoping he was being cared for properly.

    My mom became pregnant again, and this time, it was me floating around in her uterus. But something happened to my parent's relationship. Over the next few years, they would struggle to stay together and maintain a healthy family life. Richard's condition was a challenge. It also probably didn't help that my dad couldn't stay still. Felix was a man of action and was always seeking it. When he wasn't working in the factories, he was out, running craps games out of the trunk of his car or in the back rooms of the neighborhood Puerto Rican bars in Jersey City. He had a craps tarp that he would carry around in his trunk, and he knew exactly how to throw the dice in his favor.

    My dad became known as "Jersey City Felix", and he would often spend the weekends away at the horse tracks, card games, and casinos. Everybody knew my dad. Even the then-mayor of Jersey City Gerald MacCann stopped by to say hello to my dad at one of his birthday parties at The Old

San Juan Bar on Seventh and Cole Street. Later in life, he would admit to me that he valued his friends and the camaraderie he shared with them more than his family.

Nena was a fighter though, and she wasn't giving up on her family. Two months after I was born, Nena convinced my dad to get away from the streets and move to our house in Salinas, Puerto Rico. She wanted to try and live her life away from the rat race in the states and raise her family in her native home of Puerto Rico.

In 1976, my parents relocated to Salinas, settling in El Barrio Coco (Coco Neighborhood). Old sugar cane and cow pasturing fields made up this small town on the base of the Coamo mountains. It was also adjacent to a U.S. military training base named after my patriarchal name, Camp Santiago, about twenty-five miles east of Ponce. So, Mom, Eddie, and I relocated to Puerto Rico. Felix would eventually follow. His mom, my Grandmother Coca, lived in the same neighborhood and took care of me while my mom established our home and her hair salon business. My grandmother was happy to take me in. I instantly became her favorite.

Nena intended to run her own business. She installed a salon chair and station and began to establish a small clientele. Felix made it to Salinas, but not for long. Their marriage wasn't working. It also didn't help those new policies in Washington D.C. ignited the closing of many manufacturing and pharmaceutical companies on the island and sent jobs abroad to Asia. The only remaining jobs on the island seemed to be in hospitality. My dad didn't have a formal education. He dropped out of school in the

5th grade, so his tailoring skills were of no use in Puerto Rico, and his nomadic tendencies did not help the matter. His need for constant street action – and women – led him away from his husband and fatherly duties. So, as quickly as he came, he went right back to the states and left us to fend for ourselves in Puerto Rico.

After trying to make it work on her own, two years later, Mom had to rent out the houses in Salinas and relocate us back to Jersey. I can only imagine my mom being heartbroken and in need of support. The challenge of juggling two kids and an absent husband made it difficult for her to build her business.

Simultaneously, my brother Eddie began to exhibit unruly behavior, skipping school and getting into fights. It's possible that he simply needed his father around. My mom didn't desire a return to Jersey City, but she couldn't manage the challenges she faced on her own anymore. At least in the States, she could access better assistance, food stamps, and more employment opportunities. Realizing that my dad wasn't coming back, my mom sought a divorce which required her to return to the States. Reluctantly, my mom moved us back to New Jersey, a familiar place, and rented an apartment on Wayne Street in Downtown Jersey City; a temporary setback from paradise.

ADRIAN ALVARADO

CHAPTER 2

URBAN LIFE

My mom Nilda "Nena" Rivera holding my brother Richard, Barrow St. Jersey City, 1973.

It was 1981 in Downtown Jersey City. President Jimmy Carter was out after four years, and Reaganomics was on the way in. Arcades were taking over and Pac-Man fever exploded in America. MTV also made its debut. I was five years old; my big brother Eddie was thirteen and lacing up my hands with a pair of boxing gloves I had gotten for Christmas.

Boxing gloves were a rite of passage for most young Puerto Rican males. It was a way to see if any of us would be the next great Puerto Rican boxing champion like Wilfredo Benitez, who became the youngest boxing world champion at seventeen years old in the welterweight division. Getting boxing gloves became a Puerto Rican tradition. Looking back, the gloves should have come with instructions: Take these and fight your way out of here kid! Eddie and his friends had decided to start a little fight club. We were in the basement of our apartment building on 80 Wayne Street, and I was surrounded by all the kids we knew from the neighborhood. I was about to get thrown into my very first fight. One of many.

Eddie was doing his best impression of Mickey from the movie *Rocky* as he tied up my laces and gave me instructions, "Adrian, just go punch him in the face as many times as you can!" *Seems easy enough*, I thought. I just nodded my head, and at that moment, something shifted in my brain. I felt a rush of adrenaline and was laser focused. I heard the cheers and felt the energy of excitement from the kids around me. Everyone was screaming and egging us on. I didn't even think of saying no or running away. Although my opponent Little Richie was bigger than me, it didn't faze me one bit. I looked at my brother and said, "Ok, ready!"

I put my fist up, approached Little Richie and started bobbing and weaving back and forth. I began throwing wild haymakers and landed a few. The next thing I knew, Richie was huddled in a corner, shielding himself from my blows. My brother had to pull me away from him. Eddie was elated that I had held my own and won him some money. Although I didn't become the next Puerto Rican champion, after that day, I never backed down from a fair fight.

It was a year after moving back from Puerto Rico and my mother had a new man, Luis Vega. Luis, my mom, Eddie, and my newly born sister Shailin and I lived on the second floor of that 1800s Brownstone where I'd had my famous first boxing match. Luis and my mom met when we moved here; his mother, Tomasita, babysat me. My mom was rebounding, and they fell for each other, had a fling, and my sister Shailin was born in 1980. Shailin was the cutest baby, born with brown "Goldilocks"-style curly hair and big blue-green eyes.

The building had a bodega on the ground floor owned by a man named Ismael. The block was always busy with everyone's kids and adults in and out of the bodega, hanging out on stoops, and blasting salsa, especially in the warm weather. Our block was predominantly Puerto Rican, and the local factories were getting full of Puerto Rican laborers coming in from the island. My mother's main source of income came from working in a nearby factory as a seamstress as well as cutting hair part time. She would spend her Saturday mornings cutting hair in the back of Ismael's bodega.

Youngsters like me played wiffle ball in the middle of the street all the while avoiding oncoming traffic. Kids playing in the middle of the street was normal. I pretended to be Reggie Jackson from the Yankees. Us kids would spend most of our days outside on the street, playing tag, bottle caps, or skully. Skully was a popular game sometimes played in playgrounds but mostly on the streets. We would sketch a skully board with chalk on the asphalt in the middle of the street. You could play on the sidewalk if you wanted, but the asphalt on the street was much smoother than the cracked bumpy sidewalks. (Wikipedia, https://en.wikipedia.org/, n.d.)

The skully board was a large square approximately six feet on each side. Along the edge of the square are 12 smaller squares numbered one through thirteen. Then we would take the caps of milk cartons or bottles and fill them up with melted crayons, tar, or clay. Sometimes we would add a coin then fill it with clay to make it heavier for easier gliding. We would dig the tar right off the street then shave the top of the caps down a little until they almost looked like little flying saucers on the ground. The goal of the game was to hit the numbered boxes in sequence without touching the numbered box lines using your fingers to flick the caps. We would go one at a time and whoever went around the numbers the fastest won the game.

Eddie and the older kids would play quarters all the time. This was every kid's first gambling experience. It was a simple game where you threw quarters, nickels, or dimes against a wall and tried to land closest to the wall or on someone else's coin. After one round, whoever was closest would win all the quarters.

During heat waves, we would hope and pray for one of the adults to bring a monkey wrench and open a fire hydrant so we could cool off from the swampy summer Jersey humidity. One of my most vivid memories during this period on Wayne Street was splashing under the fire hydrant. My brother would get under the fire hydrant and create a huge splash like a peacock that we would all run under. He loved to splash cars as they drove by, especially any convertible that dared pass by our block while the hydrant was on. Cars would start rolling up their windows at the sight of the running water. They sometimes slowed down if they needed a rinse. Adults would sometimes join in as well. We didn't have swimming pools, but we had fire hydrants, and it brought the neighborhood together—until the fire department showed up and shut it down.

Music is a big part of Puerto Rican culture and my mom's passion for salsa dancing was undeniable. She absolutely adored it. Dancing held a special place in her heart, and she was a natural performer. Nena was always the first one on the dance floor when the salsa music started and the last to leave. She even participated in a televised dance competition as a teenager, which highlighted her talent and love for the arts.

Her love for dancing, performing, and making people around her laugh and dance, makes me wonder if my desire to be a performer may have been ingrained in my

DNA from the very beginning. The image of my mom on that dance floor, pouring her heart into the rhythm, serves as a cherished connection to her and a reminder of the shared love for the art of salsa dancing that runs in our family.

One of my mom's favorite holidays was Halloween and she utilized her sewing and makeup skills to create our costumes. She had a particular fondness for dressing me up. I vividly recall one Halloween when she transformed me into Dracula for a local party. With meticulous attention, she painted my face white, outlined it with black eyeliner, and fitted me with uncomfortable plastic Dracula teeth that made me drool. She hand-stitched a black cape with a popped-out collar and used her black eyeliner and costume paint to complete the look with a widow's peak on my forehead. Acting as my first talent agent and director, she entered me into a costume contest at a local community hall. "When you get up there wave your cape and snarl like a vampire. Make sure the crowd sees your fangs," she whispered in my ear in Spanish like a seasoned director. Following her instructions, I secured third place in the competition and won a gift basket full of wine and snacks—not the most child-friendly prize—but she was proud of me, and that was enough for me.

My mom's playful spirit extended to pranks. She would randomly dress up in costumes just to make people laugh. It did not need to be Halloween. I recall an amusing instance when she impersonated Iris Chacón, our Puerto Rican Barbie known for her tanned skin, reddish/brown hair, and curves. Iris Chacón was like the Jennifer Lopez of my mom's generation. She hosted her own show "El Show de

Iris Chacón" on Telemundo and drew in Hispanic audiences worldwide. With a mini skirt, teased hair, and paper-stuffed pants, my mom perfectly emulated Iris Chacón. Splashing on vibrant makeup, she grabbed my hand: "Vamos!" I held great admiration for my mother. To me, she resembled a movie star, and she was the most beautiful woman in the world. I always felt secure with her, appreciative that she was not only the life of the party but also the most captivating lady in the room.

For much of its history, downtown Jersey City was a shipping and manufacturing town. Industries and manufacturing always thrived in the old ports of the city. Just like its towering next-door neighbor, New York City, Jersey City has always served as a haven in the United States. The city was a melting pot of Italian, Irish, Polish, Black, Puerto Rican, Asian, and Cuban immigrants. Ellis Island and Lady Liberty were just one mile east of our apartment.

From the 1960s to 1980s, Jersey City lost 75,000 residents, which left plenty of room for us Puerto Ricans to move in. With rising crime, civil unrest, and political corruption, the city experienced a period in the 1970s that saw many of its wealthy residents leave and move to the suburbs. Before gentrification became a trend, my family resided in a prime location in Downtown Jersey City. The World Trade Center in New York City was just two train stops from us. The Grove Street Path Train Station was around the corner from our block. We had easy access to "The city that never sleeps." Jersey City and Manhattan share the Hudson River, the Holland Tunnel, and in nearby Weehawken, the Lincoln Tunnel. The George Washington Bridge lies further north in Fort Lee. (Living in Jersey City 1997-1998, n.d.)

    My mom did her best to embrace the vibrant urban life in Jersey. She relished the diverse food and cultures it provided. Chinese cuisine was a favorite, and on Sundays, we often ventured into the city to explore deals at flea markets. Taking the Path train from Grove Street to the World Trade Center, we strolled down Canal Street to Chinatown for some authentic Szechuan duck. According to my dad Felix, he experienced the best times of his life in Jersey City. But despite the City's allure, my mother held a deep yearning for her home: Puerto Rico.

CHAPTER 3

TAXATION WITHOUT REPRESENTATION:

A Brief History of The Island

Castillo San Felipe del Morro, San Juan, Puerto Rico. Also known as El Morro, is a citadel built between the 16th and 18th centuries in San Juan, Puerto Rico.

"Borinquen is the daughter, The daughter of the sea and the sun, Of the sea and the sun, Of the sea and the sun, Of the sea and the sun."
    ___*"La Borinqueña"* Manuel Fernández Juncos

ADRIAN ALVARADO

The island of Puerto Rico is about a thousand miles southeast of Miami, Florida and less than five hundred miles from the eastern coast of South America. The island is only one hundred miles long and thirty-five miles wide. It sits on the biggest volcanic fault line in the world, the Bunce Fault. If you're unfamiliar with the history of Puerto Rico, here it is in a coconut shell.

Puerto Rico was discovered by a Spanish-funded voyage at the request of the Italian mariner Cristopher Colombus, to find riches in the West Indies, now known as Southeast Asia. His arrival in the Antilles was accidental and forever changed the world. When Cristopher Colombus, crash-landed upon Hispaniola—now The Dominican Republic—he had no real idea where he was. He searched for the West Indies and thought he had arrived there. Columbus was lucky to bump into the Caribbean Islands: had he not, he would not have survived the journey around the world. Upon landing on Hispaniola, Columbus was greeted by the Arawak tribes who inhabited the island. In a letter to King Ferdinand and Queen Isabella of Spain, Columbus wrote of his experience:

> "They... brought us parrots and balls of cotton and spears and many other things, which they exchanged for the glass beads and hawks' bells. They willingly traded everything they owned. They were well built with good bodies and handsome features. They do not bear arms and

do not know them, for I showed them a sword, they took it by the edge and cut themselves out of ignorance. They have no iron. Their spears are made of cane… They would make great servants… With fifty men we could subjugate them all and make them do whatever we want" (Zinn 1980).

The Arawak greeted Columbus with the word "Taino," meaning "peace," and so he called them the Taino Indians. Eventually, by 1508, once the gold fever and depleting of resources began in the Caribbean and Puerto Rico, King Ferdinand II and Queen Isabella appointed Juan Ponce De León as the first Governor of Puerto Rico. His grandson, Juan Ponce De León II, was the first person to be born on the island and assumed governorship of Puerto Rico in 1579. His birth in Puerto Rico marked a significant point in the island's colonial history, representing the beginning of local leadership in the colonial governance structure.

Spain ruled Puerto Rico for over 400 years and after El Grito de Lares in 1868, the first revolt for independence in Puerto Rico, legislation in 1897 granted Puerto Rico the path to becoming a sovereign nation: sovereignty ended with the Spanish American War and The Treaty of Paris in 1898 when The United States took possession of Puerto Rico, Guam, and the Philippines. Despite this change in government, a considerable number of Puerto Ricans maintained a deep belief in the island's independence.

Leaders like Pedro Albizu Campos and, before him, Ramon Emeterio Betances, considered the father of the Puerto Rican independence movement, embodied the independent movement. On March 2, 1917, a month before World War I, President Woodrow Wilson signed the Jones-Shafroth Act, which designated Puerto Rico as a U.S. territory, and gave residents statutory citizenship. But this "citizenship" was a Congressional act, instead of being made part of the Constitution, and as a result, not guaranteed. Puerto Rico is considered a commonwealth of the United States—basically a colony. The residents on the island received citizenship but not the right to vote. It is like history repeating itself with the original American colonies except America is colonizing Puerto Rico. The island of Puerto Rico is taxed with no true representation in Congress or the Senate. There is a Resident Commissioner in Congress, elected by the people in Puerto Rico every four years, a role which is intended to represent us in the House of Representatives but has no voting rights. This position was established in 1900, and we still do not have a vote. (Library of Congress, n.d.)

I received my first lesson on colonialism in Puerto Rico as a young kid when I went to buy a bag of potato chips in Salinas, Puerto Rico. A bag of Wise potato chips, which cost twenty-five cents in Jersey City, was priced at forty-five cents in Puerto Rico. I remember thinking, *Damn, this sucks!* To this day, this price discrepancy still exists. On a recent trip to Salinas, I saw a pint of premium Haagen-Dazs ice cream that cost $10.99 at a local supermarket. The same pint of ice cream in Connecticut costs $4.99. If we are in fact

Americans, where is OUR "No taxation without Representation"? But I digress.

In gaining U.S. citizenship, Puerto Ricans could now join the U.S. military. However, the reality of still being colonized left a bad taste in the mouths of many Puerto Ricans on the island.

Military service is a true honor and sacrifice, but it must have been a bitter realization for many islanders to participate in the military of a new colonizing force. Had I been born in that era; I may have shared the same conflicting sentiment. I mean, how would you feel if you were about to gain your independence to then realize you are still a colony, and then had to fight in a segregated military?

Due to the small number of armed forces volunteers, in 1917 President Wilson instituted the Selected Service Act, which allowed the U.S. to mandate that men in the U.S. and in Puerto Rico to enlist. About 20,000 Puerto Rican men served in World War I, with most assigned to guard the Panama Canal. This assignment was crucial because the Panama Canal is a border—a shortcut if you will—used to transport ships from the Atlantic Ocean and Caribbean Sea to Europe and Asia. The island is also positioned to protect commercial shipments and maintain security in the Antilles Islands and the Caribbean Sea. During World War II, Puerto Rico emerged as a vital military naval base for the U.S. Army. During the Cuban Missile Crisis in October of 1962, the island was prepared for and used as a launch site, with U.S. missiles at-the-ready in case of war. Puerto Rico continues to be an essential military base. There are military training facilities throughout the island, like Camp Santiago, in my hometown of Salinas, Puerto Rico.

In the past, the island's traditional economy revolved around agriculture, with sugarcane plantations, coffee, and tobacco at its core. Even though we were a strategic military asset for the U.S. as well as deemed essential regarding the island's agricultural economy, by the middle of the twentieth century, Puerto Rico remained one of the poorest islands in the Caribbean. In May of 1947, the Puerto Rican Legislature passed the Industrial Incentives Act, which eliminated all corporate taxes to encourage U.S. investment in industry. Proposed by Senator (and future governor) Luis Muñoz Marín of the Popular Democratic Party (PPD), this Act became known as Operation Bootstrap. It helped the island and its citizens by fundamentally modernizing Puerto Rico's economy. According to Brown University's "Modern Latin America"—Juan Ruiz Toro explained:

> "Operation Bootstrap" was fundamentally about modernizing the Puerto Rican economy; because the government understood that this would only be possible through foreign investment, much of it involved providing tax exemptions to American corporations who set up shop in Puerto Rico. These corporations were then able to capitalize on the lower costs

of labor on the island, which further improved their bottom line and made doing business in Puerto Rico even more attractive... The era of change began primarily because of efforts to eradicate the island's rampant poverty, which had been exacerbated for decades by excessive dependence on agriculture. In sixteen years, the Muñoz administration successfully transformed the island's economic infrastructure and thus began Puerto Rico's modern era."

But unemployment and poor living standards remained on the island, hindering projected economic growth. Puerto Ricans had been slowly migrating to the U.S. since the late 1800s, but a large migration happened after 1945 because of those economic changes related to the transformation of the island's economy from a monocultural, or self-sustaining plantation economy, into a platform for export-production in factories. During the decade of 1940-1950, over 450,000 Puerto Ricans migrated to the mainland, including my grandparents. More details can be found at Lehman College's website on Puerto Rico's Operation Bootstrap.

ADRIAN ALVARADO

CHAPTER 4

BACK TO PARADISE

Aunt Maritza & I, roasting a pig in Salinas, Puerto Rico – 1982.

At the crack of dawn, you hear her call. Running you come to nourish your beaks. Chick, chick, chick, where have you gone?

It was 1982, gasoline cost $0.91 cents a gallon, *E.T.* was the number one movie at the box office, and Michael Jackson released his album *Thriller*, selling more than 25 million copies. I was six years old.

ADRIAN ALVARADO

My mother was getting ready to move us back to Puerto Rico, where she loved to cultivate her own food amid the lushness of the land and Caribbean Sea. There, she could enjoy the fresh fish and be part of the fruits of our little paradise—the avocado tree that graced the front courtyard, providing both nutrition and shade. The mango tree in the backyard and the green peas growing along the fence were all nurtured on her own soil. No more having to live in cold railroad apartments and paying rent to an absentee landlord who skimped on the heat in the winter months to save money. Now, my mom could give opening her hair business another shot. She aimed to create a simple Puerto Rican life for herself and her kids: this was my mom's second attempt to move back to Salinas, Puerto Rico, and make it work.

This time, she would have a new willing partner in Luis, my new stepfather. But ever since the implementation of Operation Bootstrap, many Puerto Ricans, including my family, had been migrating back and forth between the island and the States, searching for the best place to build a good life.

We were back in Puerto Rico, back to El Barrio Coco in Salinas. My mother cherished Puerto Rico, favoring the culture and warmth of her island. She longed to be her own boss, surely tired of factory work, stitching fabrics, and inhaling dye fumes for meager wages. Nena detested the cold, adored the tropical climate, and relished the flavors of our cuisine. She enjoyed speaking her native language without feeling judged for her Spanish accent in the States. Like many others, she loved being close to her birthplace, embracing everything Puerto Rico represented—culture, warmth, and home. As for me, turning six years old made it easy to adapt to my new surroundings.

    My Grandmother Coca was happy to have me back. She loved to spoil me with love, now that I was older, I could reciprocate. It probably helped that I resembled her: Grandma had light caramel skin, short wavy hair, high cheekbones, deep eyes, and a sturdy frame—built for country life. Grandma Coca was strong and well-built. Her serious glare was intimidating, and she wasn't shy about getting physical, she was quick to give a spanking to one of her children if they broke a house rule, like being late for dinner or, in the case of my aunts, having any kind of boyfriend.

    Grandma didn't remarry after she divorced my Grandfather Reuben, but she did have several baby daddies, and all her kids still lived at home. My dad's younger siblings, my aunts and uncles were in their late teens and early twenties when we moved back. They were all great and loving to me, especially my Uncle Santos, who was about seventeen at the time. He took me under his wing and would take me everywhere when he wasn't in school. I became his little sidekick.

    Santos was a huge Bruce Lee fan, and he believed he possessed similar skills and talents to the legendary martial artist. To his credit, he was a great fighter and had the respect of his peers. It also helped that at seventeen, he already stood at six-foot-three. Nobody messed with my Uncle Santos.

Uncle also loved to breed roosters for cockfights, and he showed me how he molded and made the rooster's thorns with wax to glue them on their existing small thorn and turning them into killing machines. He had his own breeding area in my grandma's huge backyard. I remember Uncle Santos taking me to cockfights with him. The arena had a rustic, makeshift appearance with a circular dirt pit surrounded by a low wood barrier to contain the birds. The atmosphere was loud and chaotic with the sound of clucking birds, shouting bettors, and the clicking of money exchanging hands.

The roosters were magnificent: huge, with rich red and yellow feathers, and some entirely white or black. They looked majestic. The owners or handlers would meet in the middle of the dirt ring, holding the roosters close enough to touch beaks, then pulling them away to tease and hype them up before releasing them to fight. As soon as they were released, the roosters would jump and attack each other with their waxed claws and sharp beaks.

It was both captivating and gruesome: the roosters were relentless, and the fight would end when there was a clear winner, usually with one rooster down, perhaps with an eye hanging out of its socket, limping, or covered in blood. If they were considered a "Gallo Fino" an "Ace," the owners would remove them before they were too badly hurt, to heal and still use them for breeding. I remember getting bored and feeling disgusted and sad for the injured roosters. Not wanting to keep witnessing the bloodbath, I would seek another kid to play with while my uncle engaged in the activity. Cockfighting was part of our cultural identity; to me, it symbolizes the grit and beauty of our history, and the pure fighting spirit of the island.

I loved it in Puerto Rico. I had an oasis of rivers and beaches as my playground. I had coconut trees to climb and many trees to pick fruit from. There was a Roman-like water canal that led from the main river in Monte Grande (The Big Mountain) and passed right through my Grandma Coca's front courtyard and through the whole neighborhood.

During weekends when my mom was occupied cutting hair filling the house up with hair spray, I'd spend my time exploring around Grandma Coca's house. The canal in front of her house where the river flowed through had clear water and I would try to catch chopas (trout) as the river carried them along. I would immerse myself in the world of our native mori vivi plants, which close when touched.

Part of the lychee family, the quenepa tree was my favorite, it bore fruits resembling large green grapes with a hard shell, offering a unique flavor. My Grandma Coca had seven quenepa trees, each named after one of her children, and I even had my own tree named after me. To access the fruity interior, you would crack the shell with your front teeth, suck on the peachy fleshy skin, and savor the rich flavor reminiscent of passion fruits. Quenepas were always a source of anxiety for mothers and grandmas when little ones were near the trees because of the fruit's large round pit posing as a choking hazard. Grandma would often remind us of the time my stepfather Luis had to use the Heimlich Maneuver to save my Grandfather Alberto from a quenepa pit stuck in his throat. The choking hazard warning applied to both kids and adults alike.

Grandma Coca maintained a beautiful garden with fruits and vegetables and embraced a self-sustaining eco-friendly way of life. Her care extended to a flock of chickens, roosters, and a pig pen. Non-recyclable waste was burned, and any food scraps and leftovers were fed to the pigs. "Pio, pio, pio, pio, pio. Pio, pio, pio, pio, pio" (Pee-oh), Grandma would sing, and all the roosters, chickens, and their little chicks would scurry and wallop to knowing it was time to eat. I would join her in tossing either left over rice or corn mix. During the weekends when I spent the night at grandma's, I would fall asleep to the sounds of her singing on her rocking chair and wake up to the continuation of her melodic tunes as she fed the chicken flock in the endless backyard. "Pio, pio, pio, pio, pio. Pio, pio, pio, pio, pio."

Grandma Coca held a prominent position of respect in the Barrio, belonging to the esteemed Santiago – Romero family. My great Grandfather, Atilano (Mayas) Santiago, was one of the town's First Selectmen. The family story is that Great Grandpa Mayas seemingly appeared from the mountains one day.

For many years I worked as a bartender and wore suspenders. I would later find out Atilano was known for wearing distinctive suspenders, just like me. I was fascinated to think that his sense of style was passed down to me. There was something tangible that connected me to my great grandfather. Despite my curiosity, I have never been able to find a photo of him, no matter how much I have asked around, but everyone tells me he looks like my dad.

Except for the eldest siblings, my dad, Felix and Aunt Sonia, all my other aunts and uncles still lived in the family home. Grandma Coca, along with her crew of four, made it work in the small, humble two-bedroom cinder-block home. There was more land than house, and there was also an abundance of love.

In her prime, Grandma Coca built a reputation as a great cook while working at the renowned Ladi's Restaurant near Salinas beach. Ladi's was famous for its stunning Caribbean Sea sunset views and for creating the Mojo Isleño sauce. This sauce, a succulent blend of slow-cooked tomatoes, onions, sweet peppers, garlic, and olives, was traditionally served over sauteed or fried fish, including grouper, red snapper, and mahi mahi. It became emblematic of the town of Salinas. Salinas is renowned for the Mojo Isleño Gastronomic Route, a coastal stretch where restaurants in Politas Beach specialize in this island mojo, serving fresh lobsters, octopus, and conch right of the boat of local fishermen.

ADRIAN ALVARADO

Every year, the town celebrates the International Island Mojo Isleño Festival which began in 2001 as a celebration of culinary identity of Salinas. This vibrant event highlights live bands covering a whole range of music throughout the evening, artisans selling their crafts, and even boxing matches featuring local talent.

Eladia Ladi Correa perfected the Canary Islands base recipe by modifying it using local ingredients. My Aunt Maritza shared that my grandmother worked at Ladi's when she was a young teenager at the peak of the mojo sauce's discovery. So, whenever my grandma cooked, you could be sure it was delicious. To this day her cooking comes up in conversations with the old timers. (discoverpuertorico.com, n.d.)

I saw all the best of our culture making an appearance during birthdays and the Christmas season in Puerto Rico. Neighbors gathered with cuatro guitars, congas, guiros, and sung plena and Christmas songs. When grandma hosted, the courtyard would fill up with neighbors. Grandma Coca reserved her plumpest pig to slaughter for such occasions. The pig was the main course. It would be prepared with all the traditional Caribbean fixings including yellow rice with chickpeas, avocado, yucca in a garlic mojo sauce and fried sweet and green plantains. And, of course, cold beer and rum! Lots of rum!

My grandmother tried her best to instill all the traditions of our culture in me, including music, food, and of course, love. This year my Aunt Maritza's birthday fell on

FLIPPING MY SCRIPT

Thanksgiving weekend, and Grandma Coca wanted me to learn how to sacrifice the pig. Killing a pig was tradition, a rite of passage and Coca wanted me to have the honor. I'm not going to lie, I found the ritual to be barbaric and unpleasant, but I would still have my fill when it was cooked.

The process began with my Aunt Maritza and a few guys holding the pig down on the table. My grandma, butcher knife in hand, volunteered my Aunt Ady to hold a bucket in place under the pig's neck to catch its blood once it was stabbed. It was essential to collect the blood that would soon gush out of the pig's neck, as it would later be used for cooking morcillas (blood sausages) which is another staple in Puerto Rican and Caribbean cuisine. In Puerto Rico, nothing goes to waste. Grandma held the butcher knife in one hand while her other hand searched for the jugular vein on the pig's neck. "Chuchin!" as she affectionately called me, "Asi!" (Like this!) she demonstrated a stabbing motion towards the pig's vein. The pig's shrieks were deafening as it was being held down and the noise seemed to intensify when I grabbed the knife. I tried to avoid its gaze, but I couldn't. Facing the pig, the thought of taking its life overwhelmed me, and I chickened out. I just couldn't do it! I could see the disappointment in my grandma's face, but she didn't waste any time, because the guys were still holding the pig down. She grabbed the butcher knife from my hand, and in one swift motion, without any thought, jammed it clean through the pig's jugular vein.

"Weeeeeeeeeeeeeeeeee!" shrieked the poor pig. I turned my face to look away.

After the pig's final squeal faded, the waterfall of blood filled the bucket. Again, to my grandmother's dismay, my Aunt Ady was holding the bucket and immediately dropped it and ran away in disgust. At least I wasn't the only disappointment that day. My grandmother became unhinged at her and cursed her name. "You goddam child get back here. How am I supposed to make the blood sausage now!" she yelled.

My Uncle Santos stepped in and grabbed the bucket. The pig was tilted to let all the blood drain out. Once drained, it was gutted from the chest to its hind legs to remove all its intestines and get cleaned. Parts of the intestines were saved for pork chitlins and then the work of marinating it thoroughly with homemade sofrito would begin. Sofrito is the base of every Puerto Rican dish. It consists of a blend of onions, garlic, green peppers, sweet red peppers, extra virgin olive oil, and recao (culantro). Marinating the pig required surgical precision. Spreading the flavors of the sofrito in all the crevasses of the pig's skin and meat and making sure every part of the pig was seasoned.

Finally, it was time for the lengthy process of roasting the homemade, home-fed, homegrown pig. Grandma had constructed a pig roasting pit from gray cinder blocks, shaped like an open rectangle with a groove for the large, thick wood roasting rod. This rod was inserted from the pig's backside and came out through its mouth. Aunt Maritza would then evenly distribute charcoal in each corner of the pit. The pig, skewered on the wooden rod, would roast in the center of the pit all day. Before the invention of mechanical turning mechanisms, the pig had to be manually rotated for 8 hours. This is where my skills came into play: Aunt Maritza would sit with me, teaching me how to turn the pig and keep an eye on it while she enjoyed her cold beer. I loved doing it.

Once the pig was fully cooked, it was chow time. When they hoisted the pig onto a table, the machete appeared, chopping through the pig like butter. The stringy, tender, and perfectly seasoned meat fell right off the bones. The first piece of crunchy skin usually went to the homeowner or a special guest. Sometimes, an eager child snatched it, but everyone got a taste of the hard tasty skin before the entire pig was chopped up for all to enjoy. My favorite part of the pig was its tail, which Grandma always saved for me. It was crunchy and delicious.

The next culinary lesson grandma attempted to teach me was the preparation of a live chicken. Although quicker, cleaner and a lot less noisy than slaughtering a pig, it was still an unpleasant experience for this city kid. In retrospect, she probably thought the pig was too ambitious and wanted to give me something smaller to kill. She hadn't lost all hope yet. Grandma Coca grabbed a chicken by its legs and neck, instructed me in Spanish to grasp its neck tightly and spin the chicken in a quick 360 circle. The goal was to disorient the chicken while quickly snapping its neck. This seemed a bit more humane but once again, I hesitated and chickened out. At that moment, my grandma realized that I was more of a lover than a butcher. Nevertheless, she loved me just the same.

I won't deny that I relished being my grandmother's favorite. She showed me a side of her not witnessed by many. Feeling safe enough to be vulnerable with me. I was her "Chuchin" (a nickname given to me at birth, which means pleasant or cute). As the youngest son of Felix, I shared his DNA, sporting light brown hair and inheriting her strong cheekbones, deep eyes, and high-arching eyebrows. I cherish memories of her holding me in her rocking chair after dinner, singing as she rocked back and forth to the rhythms of the native coquis. She would speak to me in her baby voice, telling me I was grandma's baby and kissing my face. My grandma was the best.

CHAPTER 5

EL BARRIO COCO

Our house in El Barrio Coco, Salinas, PR. The wooden house in the back was Nena's salon.

It was the fall of 1982, and I began attending first grade at Escuela Elemental Felix Garay Ortiz in Salinas, Puerto Rico. We wore uniforms, and although it wasn't a Catholic school, it certainly felt like one. If you misbehaved, teachers were permitted to spank you with rulers and paddle boards, reminiscent of the discipline I had heard nuns would administer. My start at this new school was less than ideal. During my first week, while sitting in class, I urgently needed to use the bathroom—my stomach churning as if ready to explode at any moment.

My confidence in my Spanish was shaky, and feeling like the new kid, I hesitated too long and by the time I managed to raise my hand, it was too late. "Missy, Missy, I need to go to the bathroom!" I exclaimed. As soon as she nodded with consent, I bolted from the classroom faster than Speedy Gonzales, not waiting for her to finish speaking.

The bathroom lay across the dusty courtyard. I ran, clenching my buttocks, while simultaneously fumbling with my pants buttons. I reached the bathroom just as my bowels surrendered. I didn't make it in time—my pants were soiled in front of the toilet, with liquid feces trickling down my legs. Indeed, it was a memorable, albeit embarrassing, way to start making new friends.

The school called my mom, and my stepfather Luis came to pick me up. When he showed up, I was being hosed off by the custodian, who was trying desperately to hide his laughter. I was crying and explaining to my stepdad why I shat my pants. "It's ok Pikiria" as he affectionately called me while chuckling. In the following weeks at school, I found myself constantly fending off wannabe bullies. But thanks to my Uncle Santos, those bullies messed with the wrong poo poo pants.

Just because I had pooped my pants in school didn't mean I wouldn't defend myself. I was quick to protect my space with my hands if anyone encroached upon it. Uncle Santos had taught me that if someone pushed me or invaded my personal space, I shouldn't wait to be hit—I should strike first. "Nothing good ever comes from someone being in your face, threatening you," he would say. Back then, it was hit or be hit. Fighting wasn't encouraged by any means, but it was a common way for kids, especially boys, to resolve their differences. There was no fear of major retaliation or someone returning to exact revenge. Whoever won the fight, won the argument, and that's where it ended.

My first major showdown unfolded the following week. I was hanging out with my buddy Junito, who lived just across the street from my grandmother's house. Junito and I were distant cousins, connected through my grandmother's family line. His grandmother, Modesta, was my grandmother's aunt from the Romero side. They owned a sprawling front courtyard, dominated by a massive tamarind tree, which served as our regular hangout. Here, we would play marbles and spar playfully. I often showed off the karate moves my Uncle Santos had been teaching me.

That day, Junito's grandmother Modesta had company over, so Junito and I had an extra friend to play with. He attended my school and knew about the incident where I had shat my pants. He started mocking me and my karate skills. All I remember is him challenging me and advancing as if he wanted to fight. Instinct kicked in, and I immediately performed a cartwheel towards him, landing a kick right on his nose. Blood gushed out, and he started crying for his momma. News travels fast in a small town, and by the next day, everyone at school had heard about my karate flip.

I recall another incident where my uncle's lessons proved invaluable. It happened at school with one of my classmates, Kelvin, who later became my best friend.

We were in the school's courtyard when a kid decided to pick a fight with Kelvin. Kelvin wasn't the type to back down and found himself needing to defend his ground. The opponent was no amateur; his boxing skills were evident as he skillfully ducked each of Kelvin's swings. It wasn't looking good for Kelvin, and he eventually tapped out, signaling me to take over. Now the kid's attention was directed at me. He squared up and advanced toward me. Without hesitation, I let loose a two-punch combination that landed squarely on his face. He staggered back, then came at me full tilt in a blind fury. I met his charge with a solid right, a parting shot before he acknowledged defeat. Those two fights swiftly cemented my reputation as a formidable fighter in El Barrio Coco.

Our family's roots run deep in this region of Puerto Rico. Not far from our home in Salinas was my mother's hometown of Aibonito. My parents were born in towns just twenty minutes apart. Nestled in the Sierra de Cayey, Aibonito is a mountain town perched at one of the highest points on the island, standing 2,401 feet (about 732 meters) above sea level. It is a picturesque town where the tropical, yet temperate climate remains cool and pleasant due to its altitude.

FLIPPING MY SCRIPT

There is a charming folk legend about a Spanish soldier named Diego Alvarez who, on May 17, 1615, reached the area's highest peak. Overwhelmed by the beauty of the view, he reportedly exclaimed, "Ay, que bonito," which translates to "Oh, how pretty." This tale is one of the popular stories behind the town's name, Aibonito. (Wikipedia, https://en.wikipedia.org/, n.d.)

During the Spanish-American War in 1898, a battalion comprising both Spanish and Puerto Rican soldiers managed to defeat the invading American troops due to their strategic placement high on Asomante Mountain. As the war ended, the Spanish government entered into an agreement with the United States known as The Treaty of Paris on December 10, 1898, which ceded Puerto Rico to the United States, aiding its emergence as a global power. The troops stationed on Asomante Mountain never surrendered; they would have maintained their post had it not been for the overall surrender of the island by the Spanish government in Madrid. (Library of Congress, n.d.

My mom adored her hometown of Aibonito and took us there to visit during the town's patron festival, "El Festival de las Flores" (The Festival of Flowers), which still takes place in early July and lasts for a week. Rain or shine, the bands perform their hits, and the people dance. The festival overflows with flower vendors, jewelry makers, craftsmen, and local food merchants, all operating out of quioscos (kiosks). All of Puerto Rico's gastronomic delights are at your disposal, like my personal favorites: alcapurrias, a perfectly fried meat patty made from a blend of root vegetables, yautia, and green plantains. My other favorite was called bacalaitos, a fried salted cod fritter.

My Grandmother Estelle Martinez and my Grandfather Alberto Ortiz hailed from the beautiful mountains of Aibonito, living in a municipality called Caonillas—a mountainous country village. Their house was literally built on the side of a mountain. Accessing the house by car required reversing on a one-lane dirt road downhill, because the cul-de-sac was too small and narrow to turn a car around when it was time to leave.

Grandma Estelle and my mother shared the same facial features and could have been twins except for my grandmother's brown skin and wiry black hair. My mom's hair was also black but pin straight. They both had the same small sharp nose with a slight hook at the end. Grandma Estelle was more reserved and serious compared to Grandma Coca. She liked to chain-smoke her Winston cigarettes and sit in her rocking chair. When she did let her hair down a bit, Grandma Estelle had a big, wheezy, almost breathless laugh. My grandfather Alberto had a ruddy, boyishly round freckled face. He was skinny and walked with a slight limp. He always seemed to be yelling when he talked, overcompensating for his low raspy voice which had faded after years of sipping rum like the old sailor he was.

In my grandmother Estelle's living room, there was always a picture on the wall of young Grandpa

Alberto in his navy uniform. Grandpa Alberto always had a joke, a story, and a flask of rum in his back pocket. He was funny, and he was also considered Grandma Estelle's number one pain in the ass. He loved to tease everyone, especially her. He always had a smile for me, though, and would pinch my arm, then look away and pretend he did not do it. My grandparents always seemed to be bickering at each other about something. They had a combative nature to their relationship which others in my family got a kick out of. Grandma Estelle was always annoyed by him. When I did spend a little alone time with my Grandma Estelle, she was distant, not as affectionate, a striking contrast to my Grandma Coca, who was always loving me.

All my mom's sisters still lived in Aibonito, so I got to meet all my Puerto Rican cousins on my mom's side when we visited. I found it weird, even at six years old that Grandpa Alberto and all my mom's siblings had the same last name of Ortiz except my mom who was the oldest. Her maiden name was Rivera, which she started using after she divorced my dad. That was when I started to get curious as to who my mom's dad was. The mysterious Mr. Rivera.

In retrospect, this may have been why I always felt a slight disconnect with my Aibonito brethren. I loved them, don't get me wrong: I just somehow always felt like I didn't fully belong. I connected more with my dad's siblings. They were generally more loving and affectionate. My mom's sisters were different: they were louder and more combative compared to my mom, who had a calm and more relaxed demeanor. If something went array in the family, like a fight or an argument, my mom would hold court and keep the peace, and everyone would get in line. She was always smiling and seemed to love being around her family. And me? I was just a lucky kid, playing with my cousins, enjoying the rivers, listening to the beautiful song of the coqui, and thinking things would be like this forever.

While I was busy with my adolescent adventures, my mom and stepdad Luis were trying to make it work on the island with three kids. It was 1983, and Ronald Reagan's economic policies were slowly trickling money up—not down, exacerbating the recession that gripped the U.S. economy and its colonies alike. Before long, my mom and Luis's struggles intensified.

      Luis was a good guy and a great father figure. He stood a solid 5'11", with a barrel chest and broad shoulders. He was bald on top but sported wavy curls around his scalp and always maintained either a handlebar mustache or a beard. He was born in Cayey, Puerto Rico, but Luis seemed to have already assimilated to life in the States. He found that he no longer fit into the slow island life; he was a Nuyorican now, a product of "Operation Boot Strap"—part of the wave of young men brought to the U.S. to work and fight in wars.

FLIPPING MY SCRIPT

In Puerto Rico, viable work was scarce for Luis. The island lacked trains, reliable public transit, and quick conveniences like a pizza place around the corner or a nearby Central Park. There was no Tad's Steakhouse downtown either. The agricultural jobs were dwindling; the farming life had withered away. Luis wasn't a farmer. Even jobs in the pharmaceutical factories were disappearing, moving offshore to places like China and the Philippines.

Compounding these challenges, Luis and my brother Eddie were often at odds. Eddie, navigating his teenage growing pains, was a handful. He troubled everyone, falling in with the wrong crowd and skipping school. Once, I caught Eddie behind the house smoking a joint. At the time, I didn't realize it was marijuana; I just knew smoking was bad. "Ooooh, I'm gonna tell mommy you're smoking," I threatened. His response? "Shut up! This is nothing. It's just grass, stupid." He even picked up grass from the ground, trying to convince me it was harmless. Eddie was always quick on his feet with some lies to tell.

Luis and my mom began to argue more frequently. Even as a young child, I vividly recall the palpable tension during their disagreements. My mom radiated exasperation, while Luis exhibited a stubborn unwillingness to assimilate. At six years old, already bilingual, I could catch snippets of their conversations, especially when Luis spoke in his broken English. Their arguments mostly revolved around his discontent with Puerto Rico; he claimed the island wasn't for him anymore. He complained about how Eddie was heading in the wrong direction and insisted that my mom needed to "take action." It didn't help that Eddie was also stealing from everyone, including Luis.

My big brother Eddie was the wild child of our family. Eddie was always getting into trouble and had a reputation as a bully. He was self-conscious of his now crooked left arm, which, according to Uncle Santos, he broke in three places after falling from my grandmother's mango tree as a child. Eddie was Grandma Coca's first grandson, and she helped take care of him just as she did with me.

He could never straighten his arm after that fall, leaving him with a large scar on his elbow. Beyond the physical scars, I speculate that my Grandmother Coca sensed a deeper and more troubling issue within Eddie as well. She would go silent with a stern glare and simply raise an eyebrow whenever Eddie was mentioned in conversation.

Although he was seven years my senior, I was never afraid of my big brother, but I knew he was tough. Standing 5'9" with a stout build, he was handsome, with broad shoulders and light brown hair. His eyes were hazel brown, and he had light white skin, like my mom. Eddie, a Gemini, displayed dual personalities: he could be hilarious and clownish when in good spirits, his infectious giggling laughter lighting up the room. Yet, he also had a mischievous side shadowed by dark demons. Demons he would battle with his whole life.

FLIPPING MY SCRIPT

Like my dad Felix, Luis eventually had enough of Puerto Rico and, equally, of Eddie. He preferred the urban environment, and the accessibility city life offered in the States. He loved being able to walk anywhere he wanted in Jersey and New York City, like Liberty State Park, Chinatown, and the Brooklyn Bridge.

And just like that, Luis sold his '76 Pontiac Grand Prix to fund his move back to the states. He detested having to sell that car, shedding tears as he took the money from the buyer.

Once again, my mom, Eddie, my baby sister Shailin, and I were left behind. Eddie was fourteen and increasingly more difficult to manage, and he kept skipping school. His thievery extended from us to neighbors or anyone else he could steal from, which explained why Grandma Coca didn't want him around. His habits were becoming alarmingly destructive. The last straw came when my mom was cutting hair at a neighbor's house. Glancing at the wall, she recognized a ceramic art piece she had created, adorned with mushrooms and polka dots. Curious, Mom asked the lady where she had acquired it, and the lady mentioned a young man had sold it to her. After describing him, it was clear it was her own son. The realization that Eddie was stealing from her and selling her possessions must have crushed her. In response, my mother didn't hold back; she disciplined Eddie thoroughly. While I didn't witness the punishment, I saw him afterwards, looking like a defeated, lost beat up sheep. My mom, at her wit's end, called my dad, Felix, demanding he send a plane ticket for Eddie to return to New Jersey. She insisted, "You deal with him!"

Mom did her best. She provided us with whatever the salon afforded. We frequented rivers and beaches and visited friends and family, embracing island traditions like Christmas and Three Kings Day. She taught me to place grass under my bed if I wanted the Kings to leave a gift. The first year I tried, they left me a toy racetrack, which thrilled me so much that I woke my one-year-old sister at three in the morning to tell her. Mom was not pleased that morning.

Entering second grade, I spent days in the salon with my sister while Mom worked. Unfortunately, the salon struggled financially. The local economy was no better; most folks in the neighborhood couldn't afford regular haircuts, so she often gave haircuts on credit or accepted whatever people could pay. However, generosity doesn't fill the pantry or the fridge.

I spent many hours in the loft where the TV was, often eavesdropping on the gossip and conversations from my mom's clients. Once, while cutting a man's curly Afro, he warned her about his dandruff. As she began to cut, flakes fell like snow from his head—it seemed he hadn't washed his hair in months. Mom tried to maintain her composure and not laugh, but her eyes betrayed her astonishment at the amount of dandruff. It piled into a little flake mountain on the floor, which she swept up with a mix of mild disgust and a smile.

With the salon business failing, two of her sons back in the states, and her new relationship on the rocks, Mom made the difficult decision to move us back to the States again. Grandma Coca, heartbroken by the decision, asked if she could keep me in Puerto Rico to help raise me. My mother declined the request, and so we returned to Jersey.

ADRIAN ALVARADO

CHAPTER 6

BACK TO THE FACTORIES

A view from the Empire State Building. Jersey City lies across the river to the right.

In Puerto Rico's warm embrace, my mother stood so bright, but circumstance called her to Jersey, where factories hummed at night. In Rockefeller's ghetto, with courage in her stride, she stitched our future lovingly, her heart our constant guide.

In 1984, Nancy Reagan's anti-drug campaign, 'Just Say No!' was capturing national attention as the drug war became America's longest. Meanwhile, Tina Turner pondered, 'What's Love Got to Do with It?', as the first Apple Macintosh was hitting the shelves. I was eight years old.

Upon our return to the gritty environment of Jersey City, we found shelter with my Aunt Rita. Recently divorced, Rita had relocated with her two children from Aibonito. She sported short, wavy black hair and a round face marked by a button nose. My cousin Sonia was thirteen, and Marcus was ten, only two years my senior. Rita, though often loud and grumpy, held a deep respect and love for my mom, which led her to welcome us into her home. Situated in the Downtown area of Jersey City, in a neighborhood known as The Oaks on Brunswick Street between 7th and Pavonia Avenue, Rita's residence was nestled in the Hamilton Park district, famed for its brownstone buildings. Her compact two-bedroom apartment soon became the cramped quarters for six of us, humorously echoing the old stereotype of multitudes of Puerto Ricans living together in a single apartment. While it wasn't fourteen of us, the six of us were jammed into that small space and we all awaited the day my mom could secure a job and a new apartment for our family.

Despite the cramped living conditions, my cousin Marcus and I thrived in each other's company. Marcus was tall, six feet, Afro-Latino with dark caramel skin and a dimple on his cheek. His father, Juan, like mine, hailed from Salinas, and the two had grown up together.

Marcus and I often engaged in playful fights, pretending to be characters from our favorite '80s action TV show, *The A-Team*. Marcus assumed the roles of *B.A. Baracus*, the team's muscle, famously portrayed by Mr. T, and Hannibal, the cunning leader, while I took on the personas of the charming Face and the eccentric Murdock. Conveniently located next to a park we called the oaks, we spent countless hours on the monkey bars, climbing, flipping, and pretending to save the day in episodes reminiscent of the show. Marcus, mimicking Hannibal, would pick up a stick, pretend it was a cigar, and recite the iconic line: "I love it when a plan comes together."

However, the reality was that our family's plan was far from coming together. The instability of our living arrangements made me increasingly aware of the fragility of our family structure. This was our second attempt at resettling in the states, leaving me confused about our circumstances and uncertain about the future. Despite these challenges, a glimmer of hope emerged as my mom and Luis began to communicate again. Luis would visit us at Rita's apartment, spending time with Shailin, though he never stayed. I mean where would he sleep? We were jam packed in that apartment.

Soon 1985 came along and I was nine years old. El Gran Combo's album *Innovations* topped the tropical salsa charts, *Back to the Future* dazzled cinema audiences, and British scientists uncovered a gaping hole in the ozone layer, pinning the blame on hairspray.

ADRIAN ALVARADO

We were still bunking with my Aunt Rita. At school, my young mind toggled between languages. After two years in a Spanish-speaking school—basking in mangoes, quenepas and sancocho (Puerto Rican stew), it was jarring to return to the states, to Hudson County's public schools, where lunch was peanut butter with carrots and hotdogs. I left Puerto Rico mid-second grade. Now back in the States, I was placed in an ESL class—English as a Second Language. Although Spanish still dominated my thoughts, I quickly readjusted, as kids often do. I aced my ESL class, moving smoothly back into a regular third-grade English class at Raphael De J. Cordero School Number 37 Elementary, nestled between Erie St and 9th Street in the Hamilton Park neighborhood. It was during this transformative year that the acting bug first bit me, setting the stage for my eventual pursuit of Hollywood.

One day, a short petite, cute Spanish-looking lady with a button nose and sleek, jet-black hair entered our classroom with the principal. They spoke briefly with my teacher, who then gestured towards me. Summoned to the front, I was asked if I'd like to participate in the high school play. I had just volunteered in an elementary school play about human anatomy, where I enthusiastically played the stomach, earning rave reviews. My line had been, "I'm the stomach, and when I'm hungry, I sound like this…," complete with stomach gurgles. They needed a bilingual boy from Puerto Rico, and I fit the bill perfectly. Before I knew it, I was whisked off to the high school, handed my lines, and I landed my first significant role in a play.

FLIPPING MY SCRIPT

The play, Ferris High School's Spring production of *Bienvenido Don Goyito,* penned by Manuel Mendez Ballester, revolved around a middle-aged Puerto Rican man adjusting to U.S. urban life while resisting complete assimilation. How ironic. I played Mickey, Don Goyito's young neighbor, a streetwise bi-lingual kid with scruffy knees and a beaming smile.

Ms. Maria Mateo, the brunette who introduced me to the stage, would fetch me after lunch for rehearsals, which took place in the Paul G. Brueggemeier auditorium at the high school. Surrounded by older students, I found a sense of belonging I'd never felt before. Despite our age differences, they welcomed me as "El Nene," the kid. Being in a third grader in a high school play didn't just give me a part in a play; it gave me an identity: I was an actor.

Each rehearsal began with me dirtying my knees across the stage, unknowingly practicing method acting. When the curtain rose, any nerves I might have had were overshadowed by the adrenaline of performance. I don't recall feeling anxious as I stepped out before a packed house, the auditorium's 860 seats were all filled. The bright stage lights blinded me to the audience's faces, but their laughter and engagement were palpable. That first performance sealed my love for acting and the stage. The applause during the curtain call, especially the standing ovations, was exhilarating. I felt a sense of belonging, acceptance for who I was and what I had given.

It was exciting to be part of a bilingual play in the early '80s in Jersey City. The play, which mirrored many of the audience members' lives including my own, earned us a spot in the local newspaper. The Jersey Journal featured us in an article after attending our dress rehearsal. Seeing my photo in the paper, sitting on Don Goyito's lap, both of us in traditional Puerto Rican pava (straw) hats, made me feel like a star. My mom proudly displayed that article everywhere she went, especially at her social club.

Around that time, my mom and stepdad Luis decided to give their relationship another try. Things were looking up as they found an apartment near Aunt Rita's on 7th and Division Street. My mom resumed her work at the factory, and thanks to her connections at the city council—earned through her domino games—she secured a decent job for Luis in the city's sanitation department. Luis got a CDL license and started driving whatever the city needed: salt trucks, plow trucks, you name it. He kept at it until his retirement.

    We moved into a new railroad apartment: a line of rooms connected without a hallway. The front door opened into the kitchen, which housed the only bathroom. Next came the living room, then Shailin's and my room, and finally, at the far end, my mom's room. The layout meant my mom had to pass through my bedroom to get anywhere else in the apartment, but that didn't bother me. I had my own space at last, and I loved it.

    Life was stabilizing, much like our days back on Wayne Street. Every morning, my mom woke me with a kiss and prepared cream of wheat or oatmeal for Shailin and me. Shailin, just starting kindergarten, shared the bunk beds with me. I felt big and responsible, escorting her to school each morning, just a half-mile walk. My stepdad was out early, driving sanitation trucks, while my mom headed to the factory. On weekends, we'd hang out at my mom's Puerto Rican social club, Salseros, where she and Luis played dominos or pool, have a few drinks, and listened to salsa.

I was growing up, starting to question who I was and the world around me. I wondered about my family, my parents, who my real father was, and what life was throwing at us. I was becoming aware of our social status, keenly feeling the economic disparities highlighted by television shows like *Richie Rich* and *Different Strokes*. These shows opened my eyes to what we lacked and what others had, framing my early understanding of socioeconomic differences.

Every night before bed, I would make funny faces with my sister Shai until she drifted off to sleep. I, however, would stay up, lying there staring at the ceiling with my headphones on, my mom's cigarette smoke lingering in the air as she dozed off to her novellas. My mind would race, thinking about life. Sometimes, I'd find myself missing Puerto Rico—my Grandma Coca's welcoming smile, her hearty laugh, her caramel scent. I missed climbing the quenepa tree in her yard, which was once my playground. Now replaced by the cold streets of the inner city and the morning rumbles of garbage trucks and buses.

ADRIAN ALVARADO

As sleep finally began to take over, I would recite the prayer Grandma Coca taught me: "Con Dios me acuesto, con Dios me levanto, con Dios y la Virgen y el espíritu santo, amén. (I go to bed with God, I wake up with God, with God and the Virgin and the holy spirit, amen.) I'd make the sign of the cross and drift off to sleep.

In our new apartment, things initially seemed hopeful for my mom and stepdad, but that hope was short-lived when my brother Eddie returned. My dad, Felix, couldn't handle Eddie's behavior, which was straining his new marriage to Zuleika. Eddie's troubles continued in the states, leading to school suspensions and eventually him dropping out of school at sixteen. Consequently, my dad kicked him out and sent him back to us. My mom, of course, took her son back, praying that this time it would work out between Eddie and Luis. With Eddie back, Shailin and I had to share the top bunk, while Eddie took the bottom. Most of the time, Eddie would be out all day and night. When he was home, he'd either be asleep or blasting music from his Walkman. He even had a TV, an Atari, and a Coleco Vision game console—luxuries my mom couldn't afford. My dad later admitted he felt responsible for spoiling Eddie, which perhaps led to his drug use. "I think I ruined him," he once confessed, having given Eddie large sums of money as a child, which only facilitated his fall into the wrong crowds and hard drugs like coke and heroin. We were smack in the middle of the War on Drugs, and crack cocaine was rampant in the gritty 1980s. Eddie became a victim of this epidemic.

FLIPPING MY SCRIPT

Despite Eddie's struggles, he was never mean to Shailin and me. He was always protective, funny, and loved cracking jokes. He introduced me to comedians like Freddie Prinze Jr., Richard Pryor, and Eddie Murphy. If not for his addictions, I believed Eddie could have achieved anything; he was intelligent, charismatic, handsome, and bilingual—an asset undervalued in our society, which still today often looks down on public displays of our mother tongue.

Eddie had a way with people, convincing them of almost anything. He could sell sand in the desert. I remember one time, while watching a Mets game, he bet me four dollars they'd come back to win despite being down by five in the eighth inning. I took the bet, and the Mets came back and won the game. Eddie collected his winnings the next morning, giving me my first bitter lesson about gambling.

Jersey City winters felt like a black-and-white movie compared to Puerto Rico's colorful backdrop. With no rivers or mango trees to climb, TV and movies became my escape. Eddie introduced me to the first Hispanic faces I saw on American TV—Erik Estrada on *Chips* and Ricardo Montalban on *Fantasy Island.* As a kid I assumed every Latino actor on TV was Puerto Rican. What did I know?

Mornings started with a Spanish radio station blasting the news in the kitchen while my sister and I watched cartoons like *Woody Woodpecker*, *Bugs Bunny*, and *Elmer Fudd.* After school, it was *He-Man*, *G.I. Joe*, and *Thunder Cats.* At night, if Eddie was home, we watched whatever he chose: *Cheers*, *The Honeymooners*, and reruns of *The Benny Hill Show* and *Sanford and Son.* Eddie, lounging on the couch smoking cigarettes, would tap my head, urging me to stay still while he mimicked Benny Hill's antics. I began staying up late with him, absorbing the adult humor of *Cheers* and *The Honeymooners*, which became my favorites.

On weekends, my mom would cut hair and play dominoes at her social club, Salseros, taking Shailin with her while Eddie disappeared into the city. I stayed home, indulging in morning cartoons and afternoon martial arts movies. In the summers, I would join my mom at Salseros, a vibrant hub for Puerto Ricans to celebrate their culture, owned by a couple everyone called El Viejo (the Old Man) and La Vieja (the Old Woman). My mom, always the life of the party, would snort with laughter, play dominoes, and dance.

However, things at home began to deteriorate quickly. Mom and Luis argued more, just like they had in Puerto Rico. Luis became increasingly irritated, especially about Eddie's behavior and my mom's time at the club. To escape their arguing, I'd put on Eddie's Sony Walkman cassette player when he wasn't home and lose myself in whatever music he was listening to until sleep took me. Tonight's music was Run D.M.C.'s track, "It's Tricky," from the album *King of Rock*.

I missed my Grandma Coca terribly. She'd call once a month, always bursting into laughter when I asked for her blessing. "Bendición Abuela," I'd say. She'd reply with a hearty laugh, "Ah hahahahaha! Dios te bendiga y que la Virgen te acompañe," which means God bless you and may the Virgin accompany you. One Saturday, she called with exciting news: she and my mom could send me to Puerto Rico for the summer. Thrilled, I looked forward to escaping the drama at home and returning to my favorite place in the world, where I could climb trees, eat mangoes, and live freely with my beloved Grandma Coca and Uncle Santos. This was the start of three consecutive summers spent in the haven of my grandmother's love, which remained my sanctuary through the coming turbulent years.

ADRIAN ALVARADO

CHAPTER 7

SUCKED AWAY

Luis and Shailin – 1981.

After my summer away in Puerto Rico, I returned to Jersey City and dove right back into school life. I was attending Dr. Michael Conti Public School #5 on 182 Merseles Street. My teacher that year was Ms. Oneil. Ms. Oneil and I had a turbulent relationship; she was the first teacher to start kicking me out of the classroom for acting out in class. I had begun to exhibit unruly behavior: talking during class, making jokes, and falling off my chair. I remember feeling embarrassed at times for wearing the same clothes and coming to class smelling like armpits. The energy and structure in our family life was changing.

    At nine years old, entering fifth grade, I faced a jarring episode that marked the start of another downward spiral in our household. I came home from school one day to find our door wide open, and the lock busted, inside our VCR, HBO box, and TV were stolen. I was confused and furious. Who would rob us? My brother Eddie's escalating drug issues and the shady crowd he rolled with likely had a hand in this. Or maybe Eddie did it himself, making it look like we were robbed. When my mom confronted Eddie, he fed her some line about guys claiming he owed some people money. All I knew was our home was stripped of its entertainment. What now?

    My stepdad Luis was just as exasperated. He wanted Eddie gone for good. Luis had followed my mom to Puerto Rico, taken a chance on us, and had come to love her and me as his own son. But now, my parents faced another critical juncture: it was either him or Eddie. I imagine the turmoil my mom endured—struggling to salvage her son and her marriage while juggling her roles as a wife and mother and losing on all fronts. Whether we lived in Salinas or in Jersey City, my stepfather and brother's issues were not going away. Neither were hers. Luis and

Eddie were like oil and water; they were never going to mix. My brother wasn't making it any easier with his rebellious behavior. Luis had also grown tired of my mom's involvement with the social club. Their visits there together dwindled as my mom clung to the club. She enjoyed her drinks and cigarettes. The club became her escape. Her home away from home. It wasn't my favorite place, and my sister didn't know any better. I recall many nights pulling on her arm, begging to go home.

It became apparent that her frequent visits to the club were more about seeking solace in a glass and the haze of cigarette smoke than anything else. Even though she made extra cash at the club cutting hair, the money would probably go towards paying for her drinks after. Perhaps that's why Luis began to become increasingly distant and eventually aggressive when he would drink. It was like he was channeling Dr. Jekyll and Mr. Hyde—his moods flipping on a dime.

One night was perhaps the final straw for Luis. He came to pick up Shailin and found her napping on the club's billiard's table. That sight must have been too much for him to bear. From that night onward, Luis changed. His frustrations with my mom's drinking and late nights at the club turned our home into a battleground. Arguments erupted more frequently, often escalating to the point where I had to intervene.

Despite my mom's flaws, she was still my mother. I loved her deeply, even as I watched her struggle with her demons. The club was her refuge, but it was also a trap, pulling her further away from the family she loved and the life she wanted. As much as I wanted to save her, I was just a kid, powerless against the tide that was pulling her under.

Luis was a kind and decent man and a good stepfather, and I considered him my real dad. However, Luis liked to drink himself and his temper became increasingly volatile. He began to manifest his frustration physically. One night I vividly remember returning from the social club late when Luis suddenly jumped out of his car, began berating my mom, grabbed her by the shoulders, and then forcefully rammed her back against our building's brick wall.

What followed was a horrific scene. Luis unleashed a flurry of punches on my mom, reminiscent of a boxer in the ring attacking her body, until she collapsed. It was barbaric. I was paralyzed with shock and fear, holding my sister's hand and screaming for him to stop. He eventually stopped but continued to bark at her as he shook her violently. I ran into our building's hallway screaming for help, but no one came. When I returned, I saw Luis driving away with my sister in the car. Mom was holding herself on the ground. I helped her up, trembling as we stumbled back to our apartment. That night, as I helped her out of her clothes, her pain was palpable. I could see bruises begin to appear near her ribcage, and I felt a profound sense of helplessness and shame for not being able to protect her.

A month later, another violent outburst from Luis convinced me our family might not survive. It happened on a school night. We were all at home when my mom's terrified screams echoed from their bedroom. Eddie rushed to her aid, finding Luis wielding a knife. A fierce struggle ensued, Eddie immediately grabbed Luis' wrist, trying to disarm him. I, petrified and desperate to help, grabbed a hammer from the kitchen. Together, Eddie and my mom managed to disarm Luis, who, defeated, looked on with a mixture of rage and shame. That night changed everything—our home was never the same. We were fortunate that besides the emotional trauma, the only physical damage was a small scratch on Eddies side from the blade Luis held.

I couldn't fully understand the root of Luis's violence towards my mom. I was just a kid. But the undeniable truth was clear: no man should ever lay hands on a woman. No matter what. My mom needed help, not beatings. Those incidents irreparably altered my view of Luis and the vicious cycle of this poverty mindset. Shortly after, he moved out, renting a nearby apartment on 2nd and Cole St, and sharing custody of Shailin.

In the end, it seemed Luis and mom were simply too different, each shaped by distinct dreams and a world that was pulling them apart. Nena, an island girl, was lost in a concrete jungle, seeking comfort in a place that only deepened her troubles. Meanwhile, Luis, an island boy, had transformed into a city dweller, his patience eroding with each passing day and drink.

ADRIAN ALVARADO

Despite the chaos, I still held love for Luis. He was my father figure and the man who had stepped into the role when he didn't have to. His good qualities were undeniable yet overshadowed by his darker moments. His struggle with alcohol seemed like a battle he fought alone, one that veered his relationship with my mom off course. These events shaped my views on masculinity, respect, and the proper treatment of women. I vowed never to follow in those footsteps. If ever I found myself angry enough to consider violence, I would walk away, honoring my mother and all she had endured.

The family drama eventually kept influencing my behavior at school. One day in class, Ms. Oneil was out sick, and we had a substitute teacher. Usually, when there is a substitute, everyone is just a little looser in their behavior, and so was I. As the end of class approached, I walked toward the back of the class where the closet was to retrieve my jacket. I saw a music cassette tape on the table and picked it up to look at it. It seemed like rock music. I placed it back down, not realizing that I placed it on the wrong table.

I made my way into the closet, and as soon as I entered, my classmate Jerry, an Ecuadorian kid with straight black hair that reached his shoulders, stormed into the closet, and began to push me, asking why I took his tape. Jerry was a big kid, the heaviest kid in our class. He had a big round face and must have weighed 150 lbs.

for a ten-year-old. I said that I just looked at it and put it back. He was not happy. He pushed me again, and other classmates soon got in the middle and broke everything up. I was calm at first but ticked off that I let him push me twice.

As I walked back past Jerry toward my desk, I angrily told him that if he touched me again, I was going to kick his ass. Jerry jumped out of his chair and said, "Oh yeah, kick my ass right now," and lightly shoved my shoulders again. I heard my Uncle Santos voice in my head about fights not being a shoving match and launched a right hook that connected squarely on Jerry's jaw. Jerry immediately grabbed his jaw and turned, stumbling away from me, crying. The substitute teacher sent me to the principal right away. I made my case to Principal Jackson that I only looked at the cassette tape and that Jerry was the aggressor. I told her, "All I did was defend myself." Luckily, I didn't get suspended. Principal Jackson said, "I'm not going to suspend you because God has already punished you by hurting your hand."

Despite getting a clean shot on Jerry, my hand was swollen. It was already the end of the day, so she sent me to the nurse to get my hand checked and the nurse wrapped it and said I needed an x-ray. I went home and I waited for my mother to get out of work early to take me to the medical center. Although she looked disappointed, she didn't say much to me after I explained to her what happened. My hand wasn't broken but I had to wear a splint on my middle finger for a month or so which all my classmates found amusing.

As summer approached, my mom sent me back to Puerto Rico to stay with Grandma Coca again, providing a respite from the turmoil back in Jersey.

CHAPTER 8

PARADISE LOST

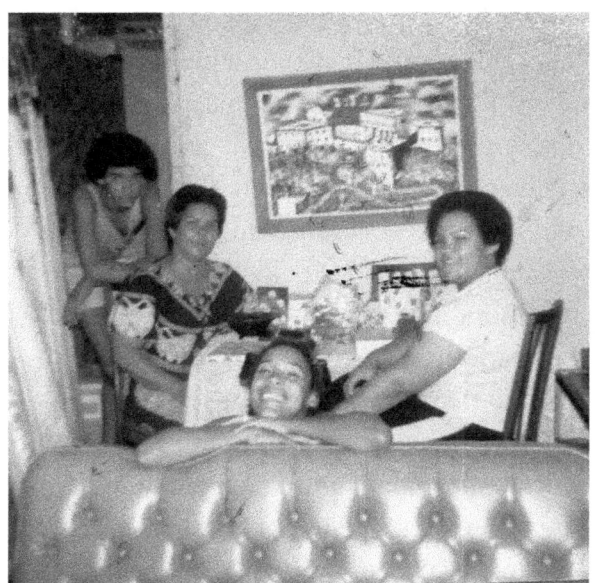

My Grandma Coca's House. Uncle Santo's top Left, Coca, Aunt Monse on couch and Aunt Maritza seated on the right.

It was 1986. The Japanese game system Nintendo made its debut. The Space Shuttle Challenger exploded 73 seconds after takeoff as my classmates and I all watched from our desks later that year. The amazing Mets won the World Series, and *Top Gun* was the highest-grossing movie of the year.

ADRIAN ALVARADO

I was ten years old and still in Puerto Rico for the summer. This would turn out to be my last summer with grandma. This summer, in particular, my grandma got me my first bike—a Mongoose BMX. I was so excited and honored; bikes weren't cheap. My grandmother lived off the land and worked part-time at the town's hospital as a custodian. I could tell that her gifting me the bike was a big deal and a sign. My Uncle Santos and my Aunt Monse, who were the youngest, both shared with me that Grandma never got Uncle Santos or any of her kids a bike. I was the first. I was the lucky one. Deep in my gut, I had the feeling that she was recruiting me to stay with her in Puerto Rico.

I rode that bike all over El Barrio Coco with my friends, exploring the whole landscape and finding dried-up sugar cane fields in Aguirre. We would ride our bikes through the trails that led us to the river. We would park our bikes and dive into the man-made wells next to the river. I always knew it was getting close for me to head back to Jersey when all my friends started school. School started earlier on the island than in the states—mid-August compared to the first week of September in Jersey. When it was getting close to the time for me to get back home to Jersey and start the school year, my mom couldn't send a return ticket for me. Word had it things were not getting any better at home. I never noticed that I lacked a return ticket on all my trips until this summer. At the end of the summer, I would always be the one to tell my grandma that I was ready to go back. When I spoke to my mom, she finally asked me if I wanted to stay in Puerto Rico. My grandma would always ask me if I wanted to stay with her as well. I would always tell her I loved her, and I loved Puerto Rico, but I needed to go back to Jersey City to help my mom and help take care of my sister. This time, my grandmother tried hard to convince me to stay with her. "Yo te voy a cuidar," she said. She promised that she would take care of me and raise me, and I could go to school there and be raised Puerto Rican.

Despite my love for her and Puerto Rico, the idea of not living with my mother never crossed my mind at the time. In my heart, I needed my mother. So, I rejected the idea of staying with my grandma permanently. Even though I was getting the feeling that my mom was trying to pass me off to my grandmother, I still wanted to go back home. I wasn't going to leave my mom alone to struggle. I was getting older and stronger and already had plans to find work and hustle and help however I could when I got back to Jersey City.

As an adult, I realized that mom probably had good reasons to try and get me to live with Grandma Coca. I'm sure she thought I was better off in Puerto Rico instead of struggling to eat in Jersey and having to deal with my brother's instability. She was probably right. At least on the island, you can sustain yourself by raising your own chickens, growing your own fruits and vegetables. I'd never go hungry or be without a stable home.

ADRIAN ALVARADO

It was a paradise lost. It hurt me to say no to my grandmother, and I'm sure she felt a little hurt as well. But when you're ten years old, you don't really understand what those types of decisions really mean and how they affect others and yourself. The one thing I knew was that if my mother was still struggling, no matter what the drama was, I had to be there to help her and my sister. Grandma was disappointed, but in the end, she scraped together whatever money she could gather and bought me a ticket back to Jersey.

I realized later in life that I inadvertently broke my Grandma Coca's heart. When I got older and began my studies as an actor, one of my college professors, Anderson Johnson, had us focus on the importance of understanding empathy and the process of connecting with it. In other words, you must try and put yourself in someone else's shoes for a moment and capture their essence and what they must be feeling or going through emotionally. When I reflect on this time with my grandma, I can almost feel the hurt she must have felt when I turned her down. In my heart, I wanted to stay with my Coca. But in the end, it wasn't about her: it was about me returning home to my mom and filling the shoes of men who were constantly letting her down. I wasn't going to be another one of those men. I was prepared to work hard and do whatever I could to be there for her, and if we were going to struggle, we were going to do it together.

As expected, every time I came back home something was different, and usually for the worse. My stepdad Luis was out of the picture for good, our phone was cut off, and our cabinets and fridge were empty. My mom was in her routine of working in the factory, barely making ends meet and living off welfare and food stamps. Eddie was getting deeper into his addiction, and he started to steal anything of value that was left around to the point where my mom couldn't send him to pay any bills because he would take the money to get high. The internet didn't exist, and online payments weren't available. With my mom working during the day, she wanted to be able to rely on Eddie to help her pay the bills and run errands, but she couldn't. Instead of helping, he was making the situation worse for all of us. I had just started the sixth grade when I came home from Puerto Rico. A week later the lights were cut off from non-payment. Instead of paying the light bill, Eddie took the money to buy drugs. I flicked all the light switches, and nothing worked. The cockroaches took charge of the house all week. *I guess that's why my mom wanted me to stay with grandma. Life in Jersey sucks* was all I could think.

    That night, I saw my mom in her candle-lit room, sitting on the edge of the bed with Eddie. Sobbing. Pleading. I was standing by her bedroom door, giving my big brother the evil eye for putting us in the dark. Eddie's face was pink from crying. He sat there with his arm around Mom, consoling her, his head hanging down sheepishly. Mom's long black hair hid the tears streaming down her face. I didn't hear everything that was said, but the conversations about Eddie's behavior were becoming repetitive, so I could paraphrase in my head what she was saying to him.

"Por favor, Eduardo. Necesito que me ayudes. Tú eres inteligente". You know better. We need you. You're inteligente, blah, blah, blah.

He didn't. *Shit!* I thought. Not only did we still not have a TV, but now we were in the dark! *I should've stayed in Puerto Rico with Grandma Coca.*

CHAPTER 9

TYPICAL

Me at 11 years old, starting to walk on the edge of the line.

"Sometimes, people are like fruits. They receive all the sweetness of the past harvest to create a tasty replication. Replication... So often one finds themselves only watching the fruit slowly grow... Never knowing anything more than how sorely important it is to be the branch... Illusions revealed. Dig into your own... Be the roots."
— *Michael Arcangel*

ADRIAN ALVARADO

It was 1987. The New York Giants defeated the Denver Broncos 39-20 in Super Bowl XXI. The first contemporary global financial crisis unfolded when the stock market crashed on a day known as "Black Monday." Bon Jovi was living on a prayer, and so was I. I was eleven years old, an honor student, and finishing the sixth grade. We still didn't have a TV. A normal home life was more and more non-existent and breaking down by the day, crumbling like old concrete.

Mom was still getting up at the crack of dawn to make us cream of wheat and remind me to make sure my sister and I got to school on time. As usual, she kissed us goodbye. Mom worked all day as a seamstress at a garment factory uptown in the Heights neighborhood, and she sometimes didn't get home till nine at night. Despite the instability at home, I was still an A-student. After school, I would drop Shailin off at the social club, where her babysitter had an apartment. When there's no one around and no entertainment at home, what do you do? Well, you hang out on the streets.

In Puerto Rico, I was like everyone else—a native, a Puertorriqueño. In Jersey City, in my neighborhood, I was considered and called a "typical Puerto Rican." Typical was the word that some local Anglos, Irish, Blacks, and Italians used to describe us. In most of their non-Latin eyes, we were all the same.

FLIPPING MY SCRIPT

Typical.

It was typical for all of us Puerto Ricans to be considered poor and on food stamps.

Typical in that my mom and dad were divorced.

Typical that I had a brother who was on drugs.

Typical that I came from a so-called "broken home."

    This narrative started to sink in, and I didn't like the script, but a lot of it was our truth at the time, and I couldn't deny that. My dad wasn't around, and my mother was always broke. I couldn't get mad at her though. She was a single mother trying to raise three kids with a minimum wage sewing job and food stamps. I never understood, and still don't understand, why my dad Felix never paid child support for Eddie, Richard, and myself. I'm not sure if my mom ever took Felix to court for child support. To my knowledge, she never received any child support payments. My stepfather Luis always took care of Shailin, but my diet started to consist of Ramen noodles and Chef Boyardee. If Chef Boyardee wasn't available, I'd have to resort to a snack I invented which consisted of raw spaghetti individually toasted over the stove. They tasted like toasted bread. When you're hungry, everything tastes good. I was also growing out of my clothes fast. My pants were highwaters, and not only were my sneakers outdated but they were also so worn out, they had multiple holes. All my mom could afford was one pair of jeans and a pair of sweatpants.

I started to rebel and look for ways to take care of myself. Increasingly I questioned why my father wasn't around. I became angry and resented him. *Why did he leave us to struggle on our own?* I remember in Puerto Rico how hard my Grandma Coca worked to teach me who my father was.

"Este es tu papa, Feliche. Mi Flaco." (This is your dad, Felix. My skinny boy.), she proudly said. In my head, I thought, W*here is he? Where is El Flaco? My dad. Why isn't he as loving as Grandma Coca? Why doesn't he look for me? Does he care about me?*

My dad's financial neglect and my mother's struggles led me to find ways to make my own money. The easiest way to make money as a kid was to smash car windows and steal their radios. All you had to do was throw a piece of ceramic rock at it. We used to get them from old car spark plugs on the street around the many local mechanic shops in Jersey City. You would smash the white ivory-looking part, the ceramic insulator, on the street or with a rock and break the large part into small pieces. Once you had a small rock-sized piece, you would throw it at a car window, which caused it to shatter instantly—and quietly. It was just a smash and grab after that.

A couple of my friends, Angel and Panchito, used to search for car stereos or purses left in cars. I heard they would occasionally find something and end up pocketing money. The rumor was that if you scored a car radio, you could sell it for thirty or forty dollars. Sometimes even more, depending on the brand. And indeed, the rumor was true; I joined my friends Angel and Panchito, broke into a car, and stole its radio. We sold it to Angel's friend, who bought it for thirty dollars. We split it three ways. With ten dollars in my pocket, I could eat a slice of pizza and have a soda every day for a week! At the end of the day, I had to figure out how to feed myself if no one else would. I did not have a tropical paradise, but I had a concrete jungle. It was either learn to survive or get eaten.

    A new mall had been recently constructed in Jersey City's Newport Harbor, with a huge, covered parking lot. We would often venture into the parking garage to cause mischief. On one occasion, we passed by a car and saw what appeared to be a large purse in the back seat. We scouted around to make sure we were in the clear. I didn't hesitate and smashed the window with my ceramic rock. I reached in and grabbed the bag. Suddenly, I heard a lady scream, "Stop, you little shits! They are breaking into my car!" I grabbed the bag and ran out of there like Speedy Gonzales. I clutched her black bag tightly in my hands like a football and kept running and dodging in between cars. I could feel my adrenaline pumping with the fear and shock of what I was doing. Angel and I ran south to the corner of 7th St. and Manilla Ave. It was already dark outside and hard to see. There was an old, abandoned elevated Conrail track there—our escape route. We climbed the rocks up to the trussell and found a safe spot where we emptied the bag's contents on the ground, shaking all the papers and folders that were inside. We rummaged through the entire bag and found nothing but school paperwork. We had stolen a schoolteacher's bag. She had a dollar and fifteen cents in change, and piles of students' completed work. Our crime didn't pay off at all that night.

    I was pissed that I had gone through all that and risked getting arrested for nothing. I hated how I felt, and I was angry at myself. That night I walked home, feeling ashamed. I came home with empty pockets, an empty apartment, and an empty stomach. At least the lights were back on, and there was a can of Chef Boyardee Beefaroni in the cabinet. Mom was able to get another TV for us, so now I could at least eat and watch TV until she came home with my sister.

    What I had just done weighed on my mind for hours. I kept thinking about how that lady screamed at me. I could still see the anger in her eyes and feel the rage in her voice. I ruined her night. Her week. I messed up the tests and homework she was going to grade. All her students' hard work wasted. She called me a little shit, and I deserved it. I felt like shit. I wanted to apologize to her. *Damn, this sucks,* I thought.

    My mind wandered to my Grandma Coca back in Puerto Rico. I wondered what she would've thought if she knew what I'd done, and what she would have thought of me if I had gotten caught. This made me even more ashamed. I didn't want to be another burden on my mother. Fuck! What did I do? I was just hungry and needed a pair of sneakers and a coat for the winter. I thought that was the only way to get it. Stealing hadn't worked for my brother Eddie so why would it work for me? This moment in my life made me realize that stealing and the street life weren't for me. I got caught up in the daily grind, but I knew that wasn't who I wanted to become. Shame was not a feeling I enjoyed or wanted to get used to. I vowed never to break into a car again. I started looking for a job, any kind of job. But there were very few jobs available for kids my age. My options were either selling weed on the corner or delivering newspapers.

The Jersey Journal recruited local kids to package and deliver their newspapers throughout the neighborhoods. I remembered my friend Jujo telling me about it. They were always looking for good paper carriers, but you had to be eleven years old to work. I was ten, but only a few months away from turning eleven. Even though I was technically too young to apply, I was tall and strong enough to appear to be twelve years old. So, I took the chance and applied.

The guy in charge of the office was Mr. Brown. He reminded me of Jabba the Hutt with his quadruple chin and big brown birthmark on the left side of his face. He was bald and weighed at least three hundred pounds. I stepped into his headquarters on Brunswick Street. between 1st and 2nd Street. I walked right up to him and told him I wanted a paper route. With his heavy breathing, Mr. Brown looked me up and down and asked, "How old are you?" I lied and told him I was eleven. He didn't really question me or ask for proof, he was fast-talking and just seemed to need bodies to work. He said, "Ok, where do you live?" I replied that I lived by Oaks in Hamilton Park. "Ok, be here Saturday morning. I need a new paper carrier for that route. I'll send you out to train with Jeffrey."

I didn't see him at first, but I knew Jeffrey. He was our neighbor when we lived with Aunt Rita on Brunswick Street. He was white, with thin blonde hair, blue eyes, and a chubby face. He used to tease me when I first got back from Puerto Rico. I recall him pulling my pants down, showing my underwear in front of everyone, and laughing. That was a thing back in those days when older kids teased you. Now I was taking over his route. Jeffrey was turning fourteen, and that was the age limit for paper carriers.

I showed up that Saturday and trained with him, learning all the houses on the route. We would show up every Saturday and Sunday morning at seven A.M. and meet at Mr. Brown's office. Our mornings started by stuffing the papers with coupons and advertisements and loading them into our metal shopping carts. If it rained or snowed, we lined the carts with thick garbage bags.

Once I completed training with Jeffrey, I proudly did my route in my old Hamilton Park neighborhood where my Aunt Rita used to live. It started on Pavonia

FLIPPING MY SCRIPT

Ave near the oaks park, then whipped around Cole and 8th Street. On Tuesdays, I had to collect the cash from our customer list between four and seven P.M. when folks were home after work. I would go through my list of customers' addresses, ring bells and knock on doors announcing, "Jersey Journal Collect." At the time, the fee was around $1.75 a week. We averaged around twenty to thirty customers, and the only way we made money was through tips. The Jersey Journal didn't pay any labor. The cash we collected went to Mr. Brown.

During my first week's collection, I made twenty-five dollars and thought I was rich. The first thing I did was give my mom ten dollars. Mom would always fight me on taking my money. She wouldn't take it and said to buy my little sister Shailin something. So, I convinced her to take the ten dollars so she could buy her something, and she took the money. Then I went to 3 Boys Pizzeria and had a feast. Shit. I have a job now, I thought. I ordered myself half a meatball parmesan sub with a large root beer for three dollars, and I also asked for four quarters for the arcades. I ate like a king and had my fill on the Donkey Kong Jr. arcade game.

Unfortunately, my paper route wasn't consistent enough. It became a hassle to collect money from the customers. They never seemed to be home on collection day. If they were home, most would ignore me until I left. My route only lasted a few months. Soon enough, my pizza and arcade money ran out, and it was time for me to find another hustle.

ADRIAN ALVARADO

My mother kept getting deeper and deeper in the hole—she just couldn't keep up financially. My brother Eddie wasn't around much, and he wasn't contributing anything other than endless headaches for Mom. Eventually, Mom couldn't keep up with the rent. Welfare only paid for food, and half the time, she had to exchange the food stamps for cash at a fifty percent markdown. Simultaneously, she didn't seem to have much work. I knew things started getting serious when, a week or so later, we arrived home late from the social club to find the landlord had put a padlock on our door and locked us out.

Mom stood at the door just staring at it, in shock, holding my little sister Shailin's hand. She looked broken. Unsure of what to do. *This is different. Now what?* I thought. After seeing my mom's face and the look of despair, I knew I had to find a way inside. I quickly had an idea and told my mom that I could get us inside the apartment. I knew how to break into the apartment in an emergency. It wouldn't be the first time I had to do it, so I was confident that we weren't going to be homeless. Not tonight, anyway. I ran down the stairs and outside our building.

Next door to our building there was a one-story mechanic shop that was easy to climb using the commercial garbage dumpster they had by the entrance. I had climbed it before with my friend Jujo who lived downstairs from us. We used to get up on their roof just for fun when we played in front of our building. I jumped on the dumpster using my ninja skills, and I climbed onto the roof of the garage. I then walked along the roof until I got to the front of the building on Division Street. The buildings were connected, so it was easy to reach our fire escape from the roof. I then reached and jumped into the first-floor fire escape. Moving quickly and quietly to not disturb our first-floor neighbors, I quietly reached the window of our apartment. I knew we never locked our fire escape window because that was my mom's smoking spot. I opened the window, and I was in.

Our landlord must have forgotten the uniqueness of a railroad apartment, they have two entrances. We had a back door which he didn't padlock. It had an interior lock that you could only open from my mom's bedroom. This is how I let my mom and sister in, and the only reason we could sleep in our beds that night.

In my bed, staring up at the ceiling, I recall feeling proud that I was there to help my mom and siter that night. But consistently breaking into our apartment only lasted for a few weeks before we had to move out. Mom found a small, one-room studio apartment from a friend who owned a building on Coles Street, between 2nd and 3rd Street. It was above his bodega called Santos Bodega. The studio had a small kitchen and a small bathroom. My mom, Shailin, and I slept on mattresses we laid on the floor because most of our furniture was in storage because of the lack of space. Eddie would crash occasionally. As usual, he would disappear for days or weeks at a time and then suddenly reappear. Mom said our living arrangement was just temporary while we

ADRIAN ALVARADO

waited for Section 8 housing assistance to help us find a bigger, more comfortable apartment.

CHAPTER 10

JERSEY CITY FELIX

Felix Alvarado – 20 years old

She said, "This man is your father." Who? My father? That man? Really? This man is my father? But who is he? Do you know him? Does he know me? Does he know I'm his son? You say he's my father, so make me understand.

ADRIAN ALVARADO

Felix Alvarado Santiago was born in Salinas, Puerto Rico in 1947 to Ruben Alvarado and my fourteen-year-old grandmother, Atilana Coca Santiago. My great-great-grandparents, as well as most of the newly established coastal communities, were originally from the central mountains of Puerto Rico, a township called Coamo, founded by the Spanish conquistadors in 1579. After the Spanish-American War, US military bases were established across the island, including our mountainous region of Coamo, forcing a migration south to the coast of Salinas. My grandmother's house stands less than a half mile from the fences of the Camp Santiago Military Base—an area where they still burn fields, shoot, test weapons, and perform military operations today.

There are many stories about Camp Santiago. I was told by Grandma Coca that one of her older brothers was blown to bits by a landmine in Camp Santiago's training fields. To make some side money, the locals would sneak into the training grounds to steal triggered landmine remnants. The island was fertile ground for US military experiments. My Grandfather, Ruben Alvarado, served in World War II. When he returned, Ruben and Coca got married, had my dad, and moved to Jersey City where they had another daughter, Sonia.

My Grandfather Ruben made a living working in restaurants as a bartender and server. The only picture I have of my grandfather is of him as a young man standing behind a Jersey City bar with his brother Alfonso, called Sloppy

Joe's. In the picture, he's sporting a thin mustache with a cynical smile and a short-sleeved collar shirt. He had light blue eyes, wavy hair, a cleft chin, high cheekbones, and a strong forehead like me. But my grandfather wasn't a good husband or father. Whatever a man said in his household at the time was law. If you didn't listen, you got slapped or punched. My father once recalled how his dad and his uncles were brutes, always quick to smack him in the head for something he did or didn't do.

I met my paternal grandfather by chance on the NJ PATH train. I was heading to New York City with Eddie. It was a strange coincidence that I met my grandfather before I even met my father. Usually, when Eddie and I went into the city, it was to buy school clothes for me on Fourteenth Street in midtown Manhattan, where they had a strip of low-cost clothing stores. My mom would make me hold the money of course. We got on the train and suddenly Eddie stopped and noticed someone. He pointed him out and introduced me to him.

"Ruben, this is Adrian, Feliche's son," Eddie told him. Then, Eddie casually said to me, "This is your Grandfather Ruben, Feliche's dad." My brother never called our mom and dad "mom" and "dad." He always referred to them by their nicknames, Nena and Feliche (Feh-lee-che), as well as all our relatives. All I remember that day on the train is that I was mesmerized by meeting my grandfather. There he was. My oldest living ancestor. My namesake, Alvarado. He was short, 5'7" or so, and he had short, cotton-like wavy hair that was completely white, like the world-famous

ADRIAN ALVARADO

Puerto Rican percussionists Tito Puente. He had a button nose and wore thin round glasses, and his blue eyes popped behind the lenses. Eddie was talking to him, and Ruben just nodded and looked at me briefly. Didn't say anything to me or ask me anything. Didn't pat me on the head or back. He didn't ask me how old I was or smile at me or show any interest in meeting me at all. He just nodded his head at me, casually, and they finished their talk. He got off at the at the World Trade Center station as if nothing had happened. He was on his way to play the New York lottery, according to Eddie.

I was shocked. I had just met my paternal grandfather for the first time by chance, on the train, he looked at me like I was a stranger that he didn't care for. I felt very strange. Despite feeling confused and angered by his unspoken dismissal, internally I still longed to talk to him, just like I longed to talk to my dad. The image of his face kept running through my mind, cementing his features. It seems only normal to want to have a connection to my paternal side. I didn't know it or understand the importance of it at the time, but I felt it. I would see my grandfather one other time on that same train. I was a few years older, heading into the city for something, and there he was, waiting for his stop. I just stared at him. I didn't have the courage to say hello. My fear of rejection was too great. We just sat in the same train car as strangers. While I knew who he was, he didn't know me. I wished I'd had the courage to say something that day. Perhaps things would have been different, who knows. But he had a chance to bring me in the first time we met. *Why didn't he? Why was he so distant? Why wouldn't he want to meet his first-born son's son?* I thought. Questions I was too afraid to ask at that moment. I was afraid of feeling rejected again. I mean, what do you say? Hey, I'm your grandson. Remember me? I figured, if he wasn't interested in me, why should I be interested in him.

Later, as I got to know my father, I would begin to piece together why my grandfather looked at me the way he did. To put it simply, I believe that some people, even if they are your family, simply don't ever understand or experience love and will never have love within them. What else could it be? As a father or a mother, how could you not want to connect to your namesake, your children?

My father dropped out of school in the sixth grade after his parents' divorce. It was a different time in the countryside of Puerto Rico in the 1950s. It was common for kids in rural townships to go to school barefoot, and he was one of them. He would tell me that school wasn't for him, he liked to play card games. When he went to school, he went in one door and came out of the other. Then at 18, he attempted to join the military in Newark, NJ, and was put right back on the bus home because of his flat feet and probably his lack of education. When plan A joining the military didn't work out, plan B came into action. Felix was going to play the lead in his own movie, a Puerto Rican without a cause, the big boss, a rolling stone, echoing the sentiments of the song by The Temptations. My dad shifted his focus from becoming a soldier to becoming the best hustler in the world, starting in Jersey City.

"I love action!" he said to me once in his thick Puerto Rican accent. My dad would eventually tell me stories about being at some of the most historic events in sports history, like at the Belmont Stakes Racetrack when Secretariat won the triple crown in 1973. He stood on a garbage can top of on the sidelines, watching the race. He swore up and down that you could see him in some of the vintage footage. "I was the only Puerto Rican standing on a garbage can," he'd exclaim with a sense of pride. He'd argue with anybody that the greatest of all time was Muhammed Ali. "The only time I cried for an athlete was when he died," he said to me. "Ali was the best!"

Felix also loved the New York Yankees. He first arrived in New York on his own when he was seventeen years old. He landed in the Bronx with his roommate and my future Godfather, Roberto Acosta. They lived right next to Yankee Stadium before they moved and ended up in Jersey City. My dad hated the Mets because in 1973, he bet our rent on the heavily favored Cincinnati Reds, "Big Red Machine," to beat the Mets in the NLCS. The amazing Mets beat and shocked the Reds in five games. My dad, the consummate gambler, lost the rent. For as long as I could remember, he said, "I don't want to know anything about those cabrones (bastards)!" when referring to the Mets. To help me understand my dad, I had to go back to the beginning.

It begins when my grandparents Ruben and Coca's relationship ended; the story goes that my grandfather's blue eyes didn't count on my grandma's right hook. Coca wasn't someone to mess with. She had heavy hands and wasn't afraid to use them if she needed to. She didn't take shit from anyone. She decked my grandfather right back when he tried to get physical with her. Domestic violence in those days was not uncommon in many households. Soon, Grandma packed her bags and was back in Puerto Rico with my dad and Aunt Sonia. This led to a bitter custody battle, but in the end, my grandma won custody. She moved to Old San Juan after her divorce and began working in restaurants and bars. My dad Felix grabbed a shoebox and shined shoes on the corner of Calle Luna in Old San Juan, where my grandma had an apartment. My Aunt Maritza was born there.

The 500-year-old cobblestone streets of Old San Juan was where my dad Felix started to learn about life and how to hustle. He told me how his grandfather, my great-grandfather Mayas, taught him card tricks and games. He hung around the old-timers, and they taught him how to hold and throw loaded dice. They showed him how to play cards, mark them, and how to spot them. There was a period when Grandma Coca was a bit of a wild child after her divorce and got caught up working in restaurants and bars. At one point, she left my dad and his sister Sonia in Salinas with my great-grandmother Julia to live and work in Old San Juan's Calle Luna. When my grandmother fell in love, she would fall hard. This feeling of abandonment left my dad bitter with his parents' relationships for life. These are the events that happened in our family that no one talks about—what I call untold family history. These events led to my dad eventually leaving on his own for the states as soon as he could.

I'm not sure why my mom never talked about my dad to me. The first time I really heard my father's name was when my mother sent my troubled older brother Eddie to live with him in Jersey City when we were still in Puerto Rico. It was Grandma Coca who always reminded me of who my father was. I remember her making excuses for him not being around. I was only two months old when he left for good, and I had no memory of him as a child. Later in life, my dad would confess to me how my mom pleaded with him to stay with her and the kids. He told me how he stared at me in my crib in our house in Salinas and how I stared back at him. But that wasn't enough to make him stay. He didn't seem to have the paternal instinct to stay and raise his sons. According to him, he was "loco," crazy. Too busy chasing ghosts. He couldn't stay still, so he left.

After leaving my mom, he met a Cuban beauty in Miami in one of his gambling escapades. Two years later, Felix had another daughter—my half-sister Rosa. I guess that officially signified the end of my parents' relationship.

I was ten years old when I officially remember meeting my dad. It was shortly after I came back from my last summer in Puerto Rico. My mom and I were standing on Brunswick and 5th Street in front of the Salseros Social Club. Suddenly, I saw a skinny man with short, curly black hair sporting a goatee swaying towards us and flashing a big toothy smile. "Que Paso?" (What's happening?) he said to my mom. Then, he walked towards me and patted me on the head and shoulders and asked, "Adrian, estás bien?" (Adrian, are you good?).

I sheepishly cuddled next to my mom's hip, feeling her long thin hair on my face, and nodded, unsure how to react. My mom said, "Say hi to your father, Felix." I was fascinated by his face, studying all his expressions and mannerisms, looking for myself in him. I shook his hand, and, in my head, I thought, *This is my dad? The man? The myth? El Flaco?* I felt a mix of emotions.

My dad had a way about him, he stood at 5'11" and talked loud and confidently with a hint of sarcasm. He and my mom chatted for a bit. I clearly remember her body language when they were talking. She had her arms crossed and her head high and didn't maintain eye contact with him when she spoke to him. I couldn't help but stare at them. This was the first time I'd ever seen my parents standing next to each other, ever, and unbeknownst to me it would be the last time. Then I heard my dad say to me in his thick Puerto Rican accent, "Adrian, you want to come live with me?"

I looked up at my mother, like, A*re you really gonna let him take me away?* I thought to myself, *Does she want to pass me off to my dad now? I just met the man!*

She said in Spanish, "It's up to him if he wants to live with you. He's your son. Adrian, do you want to live with your father?" she asked me. I was surprised by her question. I thought, *Is she serious? Is she okay with letting me go?* I couldn't just decide then and there to live with a man I had never met. Even if he was my father. He was a myth in my mind, the skinny man my grandma spoke of. I shook my head no.

He let out a big laugh and said, "It's okay. You can tell Eduardo to bring you to see me at my apartment, or you can visit me at the Old San Juan bar on 7th Street."

He reached into his pocket and pulled out a huge knot of cash wrapped in a rubber band. My eyes popped out in awe of his cash. I had never seen a knot of cash that big. Now I was really confused. *My dad's got money? We were always struggling,* I thought. He peeled off a ten-dollar bill like it was nothing and gave it to me before he walked away towards 7th Street. This was my first child support payment.

The following weekend I went to visit him for the first time with Eddie in his new apartment. Dad had a one-bedroom uptown on Jordan Ave in Jersey City, off Montgomery Blvd. Just 10 minutes from our apartment. He was living with his new bride Zuleika, Zuly for short, and he was a father again. Number five was my new baby sister Zulisha.

That morning Eddie and I started walking up Newark Ave on our way to visit my dad when suddenly he pulled a joint out of his pocket and lit it up. He then stopped and dropped his hands and arms behind his head, falling on the sidewalk into a backward bridge position. He was showing off his breakdancing skills and showing me how to get higher by smoking and holding the smoke in your lungs while being upside down. He stood up, exhaled, and said, "This is how you do it, bro." He then asked me if I wanted some, and I just stared at him. He shot back, "What, are you scared?" I had my way of just ignoring my brother when he was being pushy. I never took him seriously and somehow already knew I was more mentally sound and mature than he was. Nancy Reagan's slogan popped into my head, and I just said "No." I knew the headaches he was causing my mother because of drugs, and I didn't want to add to that. I wasn't tempted by it. I shook my head and kept walking.

I was nervous about hanging out with my dad. When we got to their apartment building, we were buzzed up. Zuly opened the door and greeted us. Zuly, with her long curly black hair and freckled face, was very pretty with high cheekbones, a shapely slim build, and a vibrant personality. Suddenly, I heard a loud nasally voice saying, "Que paso?" (What's happening?)

There he was, grandma's Flaco, my father, he walked up to us with a smile. Here he was, living a domesticated life—a life I always wanted with him and my mom. It was surreal. I didn't really know what to make of it at the time. I was just glad to have found my dad. I remember I felt at home with my dad and Zuly, playing with my new little sister Zulisha, and watching the Kung Fu flicks on tv while they talked and ate in the kitchen. I remember how my dad came out after lunch and performed a couple of card tricks for us. He would stand next to me and pat my head and ask me in Spanish, "Estas bien?" (You good?). I would just sheepishly shrug. He would then reach into his pocket, pull out that knot of cash again and peel off a ten-dollar bill, and hand it to me. My brother Eddie was always quick to reach out his hand

and ask for his cut. "I'm the oldest so you gotta give me double." Eddie was quick to say. My dad laughed.

Walking back home, I recall feeling happy that I had finally connected with my father. That I could easily walk up the hill and be with him. After that visit, I would start visiting them on my own here and there, and I would even spend the occasional weekend at their apartment.

As I reflect, I find it befalling and amazing how geographically close my father and grandfather had always been to me. I mean, we all lived in Jersey City. My father literally lived just ten minutes from our apartment. Yet, in my mind, when I stayed up all those nights thinking about how the men in my family weren't in my life, it felt like they were a thousand miles away.

Even though I could visit my dad now, he was barely ever there. My time consisted of visiting and spending time with Zuly and my baby sister Zulisha. Zuly would take me shopping and buy me what I needed for the winter season. She became a great stepmother. It seemed like my dad would be out all weekend and show up on Sunday to chill in bed, relaxing and resting from his weekend-long adventures, reading the Sunday New York Daily News, and watching the NY Giants play football.

One thing I learned about my dad during my visits was that he had some great cooking skills. The first time he made paella for me, it was the best meal I'd ever tasted. The story goes that while Dad was with his Grandma Julia, my great-grandmother, she taught him how to cook. She also gave him some sage advice. I'm paraphrasing here, but it went something like: "Learn how to cook because you're going to be alone sometimes, and you don't want to depend on a woman or a restaurant for a good meal."

To my dad's credit, he was consistent. He didn't pretend to be anything but himself. What you saw is what you got with Jersey City Felix—a straight-talking lover and hustler. When my dad wasn't hustling, he still made a living as a tailor's assistant working in the garment districts. Zuly was just out of the army reserves and was in school studying accounting. I remember when I would visit them how she would spend her time telling me about my dad and our family history, practicing her typing on a typewriter on the kitchen table. I didn't mind that my dad wasn't there most of the time. I found solace in the fact that I had a new haven. My dad and Zuly's place. If I felt like I didn't want to be alone in our cold apartment or mom's social club, I had another place to go—a home where, if I was hungry, I knew I had a warm meal waiting for me. Zuly was kind and treated me with love, like I was her own son.

But I'm not going to lie; I still had daddy issues. My feelings toward my dad were naturally conflicted. Despite spending time at his apartment, he remained a distant stranger. As I pieced together the puzzle of his absence, I experienced bursts of anger towards him for not being there—a "typical" absent dad. At that age, I couldn't fully comprehend why a man wouldn't want to be around his son. I didn't know how to express my feelings to him; instead, I kept all my anger and frustration bottled up inside.

ADRIAN ALVARADO

Even though my dad was partially in my life, my mom was still struggling. Felix had his family, and they both worked like everyone else during the week. My brother eventually got into the pattern of getting arrested. He did time here and there for things like jumping the turnstile on the subways, shoplifting, and who knows what else. They sent him to the Hudson County Correctional Facility in Kearny, New Jersey. My mom was struggling to provide basic needs for us. I wanted to help. But how could I? Making a dollar wasn't easy at eleven years old and I wasn't going to start selling drugs or get into a life of crime. In the 80s, you were encouraged to hustle and make money as soon as you could. Any way you could. Especially if you're poor. But now, I had a new ace in my pocket. My dad.

It was a real blessing that my dad came back into my life when he did; during the time when my mother was struggling the most. I think she knew that she had no other choice than to put her pride aside and reach out to him for support. I started to go look for him whenever I needed cash on a regular basis at the Old San Juan Bar, or Guillos Bar, his two favorite hangouts.

The Old San Juan Bar was on the corner of 7th and Cole Street in Downtown Jersey City. A rustic hole in the wall, as the saying goes. The first time I stepped foot in the Old San Juan Bar was in 1987; I was eleven years old. The bar was just four blocks from our apartment on 7th and Division. Of course, I was hungry and needed to eat, so I walked into the bar and popped my head in. The bartender, with his head on a swivel, turned to me right away and asked what I wanted. I stared at him and said in Spanish, "Estoy buscando a Feliche. Soy su hijo, Adrian." (I'm looking for Felix, I'm his son, Adrian).

The bartender looked at my face and knew I wasn't lying. I was my father's son. I never realized how much I resembled my dad until I started looking for him. The bartender waved me in and pointed at the back door. I made my way through the dark smoke-filled room full of Puerto Ricans, Dominicans, Cubans—all kinds of "ans"—hanging out and socializing. I walked through the door to find another door, which led to a small room. The room was brighter but tiny, barely fitting the table and chairs inside of it. It smelled like cigarettes and liquor. All the old-timers at the table looked just like that famous painting of dogs playing cards, smoking, and drinking. But instead of the table being full of dogs and chips, it was full of Puerto Ricans, cash, ashtrays filled with cigarettes, and drinking glasses all over.

I spotted my dad sitting in a chair in the middle of the table facing the door with one arm tucked behind the chair and a stack of cash and cards laid out in front of him. When he saw me walking in, his eyes opened wide—he was surprised to see me. He shined his big toothy grin at me and called me over. He pulled me next to him and told the table and everyone in the room, "Esté es mi hijo, Adrian." (This is my son, Adrian).

And there it was. He said it. "He's, my son!" My dad said I was his son. I had never heard those words in my life.

I remember smiling when he introduced me. I finally felt like I was a part of him. Like I belonged to him. I didn't realize until that moment how much I needed to hear those words. He asked me if I was okay, and I shrugged my shoulders bashfully. I wasn't okay. I was hungry, and there was nothing to eat at the house. He reached for the stack of cash in front of him and peeled off a ten-dollar bill. "Go get something to eat." he said.

My eyes opened wide, and I grabbed that bill quicker than Speedy Gonzales. My dad invited me to visit him at the apartment the following weekend, and I eagerly agreed. I thanked him and said goodbye to everyone at the table. I walked outside elated—I was going to eat well and get me a slice of pizza, even play some arcades.

That night changed my life forever. That's the night I felt like I truly found my dad. He was within my reach. I was his son, and he was my father. I could go to him, and he would receive me if I needed him. That was also the night I met Tony Conte.

CHAPTER 11

A DOLLAR IN YOUR POCKET

A view from the counter of Tony's Pizzeria.

"Give a man a fish, and you feed him for a day; teach a man to fish and you feed him for a lifetime".

The proverb is often attributed to Chinese philosopher Lao Tzu.

After leaving my dad at the Old San Juan Bar with my newfound cash, I headed straight to 3 Boys from Italy Pizzeria on Monmouth Street to grab a slice of pizza and play a couple of rounds of Mario Bros arcade—my two favorite things to do.

Patsy, the owner, was in his mid-fifties and owned the building, with three apartments upstairs. Patsy was portly and had an old-world Italian look. He stood about 5'6," and was half bald with a slight combover and a round face. He spoke with a thick Italian accent. Patsy immigrated here with his two brothers, who had their own pizzerias in nearby Hoboken. The family prospered in America. Patsy retired from making pizza himself and began to lease his pizzeria. A guy named Vincenzo had taken over 3 Boys but tonight, instead of Vincenzo being behind the counter, it was Tony Conte running the place. Tony was a twenty-two-year-old Italian American who grew up around the corner from the pizzeria. He had black wavy hair which he combed back and sported a big smile and glasses. Tony was short, barely five feet tall. He was a spitting image of the actor Danny DeVito but with hair. Whatever Tony might've lacked in height, he made up for with heart and his stocky muscular build. He was a bodybuilder in his teens.

When you entered 3 Boys Pizzeria, the counter, pizza station and oven were on the right. It had a small dining room in the back of the pizzeria that had a few tables, two arcades, and a pinball machine with a little prep kitchen behind it. I ordered a slice of pizza with a small soda and four quarters for the arcade. While enjoying my slice, I overheard Tony engaging in a conversation with a customer by the counter. He was sharing his aspiration to launch his own venture, saying that he was assisting Vincenzo due to his inability to cover the rent at 3 Boys.

In fact, Vincenzo was working for another pizzeria to make ends meet and help cover the rent. Tony came in to help with the intent to take over when Vincenzo's lease was up. He said to the customer that he was doing his best to negotiate with Patsy, the owner, so he could take over, but Patsy was not willing to negotiate on the rent and would rather keep the pizzeria closed. Tony called his bluff and said he would open his own place. He could've opened it anywhere in the city but decided to open another pizzeria right next door to Patsy's. Listening and assessing was one of my strongest skills. When I heard this, I saw it as an opportunity to introduce myself. I didn't care about any of the drama—I just wanted a job. I walked straight up to Tony on my way out and said, "What's up? My name is Chino. I heard you're opening your own pizzeria. I'm looking for work. I'm a good artist, and I can help draw 'coming soon' signs for your opening." Tony looked at me up and down with a who the hell is this kid kind of a look and said, "Really? You're an artist, huh? Ok, I like that. You're a hustler. How old are you?" I said, "I'm eleven, but I'm going to be twelve soon."

Tony was so impressed by my drive that he hired me on the spot and commissioned me to draw him a sign. He told me to show him what I could do and bring it to him the next day. I went home right away and started to draw an 8x10 flier with a pizza man flipping a pizza with the words: "Coming Soon! Tony's Famous Pizzeria!"

The next day, I brought him the flier. Tony liked it, made copies for me, and asked me to distribute them and put them on the car windshields around the neighborhood. That was my first paying job for Tony—he gave me five bucks. Soon after, Vincenzo did have to close and give up his lease. Patsy did not budge and left 3 Boys Pizzeria closed. Now that 3 Boys Pizzeria was closed, Tony, a stubborn Italian himself, kept his word and planned to open his place next door. I gladly became his errand boy.

I personally witnessed the conversation that started what was to be known as "The Jersey City Pizza Wars." I was standing on the sidewalk with Tony in front of his future pizza shop, which was under construction when Patsy walked by on his way to his building next door. They were both standing on the sidewalk. Patsy had a copy of the flier I had drawn for Tony in his hand. He had a mocking smile on his face like he found it amusing. It seemed like he thought Tony was joking.

Patsy stopped Tony and mumbled a few words to him in his thick Italian accent. I couldn't make out what they were saying to each other, but Tony later filled us all in. Patsy told him he was planning to reopen his pizzeria, 3 Boys, and he muttered to Tony, "I'm going to take the shirt off your back."

FLIPPING MY SCRIPT

Tony took that as a challenge, and they shook hands. Now, we were going to have two pizzerias on the same block, right next door to each other. A pizza party on the block. They were neighbors. 3 Boys from Italy Pizzeria's address was 415 Monmouth Street, and Tony's Famous Pizzeria's address was 415 ½ Monmouth Street. This would later create a divide between the neighborhood between the old-school loyal customers of 3 Boys and Tony's new clientele. When Tony started construction on his pizza shop, he asked me to help. Of course, I said, "Hell yeah!"

I started showing up at the pizza shop every day after school to help in any way I could. It was better than being at the social club with my mom, at home by myself, or on the streets. I was a gopher for whatever Tony and his brother Bobby needed. I would keep the place clean, sweeping and gathering the garbage while Tony and Bobby worked on construction. The brothers built most of the place. Bobby was a do-it-yourself kind of guy. He was a Home Depot freak and had all the tools needed for the job. I did a little construction as well. I helped scrub the glue on the wallpaper, and they would put it up. Tony wasn't paying me for any of this, and I didn't ask for any money; I saw this as my way in. A way to earn a job when he opened the pizza shop. When I asked Tony if I could have a job when he opened, he said, "Of course, Chino. You're going to be my left arm." Tony still gave me a few bucks here and there and said I had a job with him forever.

ADRIAN ALVARADO

We built the pizza shop from scratch, and I was excited to be a part of the process. Soon, Tony's Famous Pizzeria opened, and I had my second job at twelve years old. More importantly, I had a consistent food source for my family and myself. There would be no more going hungry thanks to Tony and his Pizzeria.

CHAPTER 12

PIZZA MAN

Me, slinging the sauce at Tony's Pizzeria. That's my little sister Shailin in the picture frame behind me.

It was 1989. *Batman* starring Jack Nicholson and Michael Keaton was released. George H. Bush defeated the bushy-eyebrowed Democratic candidate Robert Dukakis for the Presidency, and Bobby McFerrin's "Don't Worry Be Happy" was the song of the year.

ADRIAN ALVARADO

Tony's Famous Pizzeria opened with rave reviews. Patsy from 3 Boys was still closed but being remodeled. Tony's Famous Pizzeria was the only game in the neighborhood. When Tony first opened, everyone supported him. He was a local kid with new ambitions and goals. Tony was likable and generous with what he had. He fit right into the neighborhood, which wasn't perfect, but it was ours. Patsy was the old guard who had already made his money.

I was thirteen and kept showing up to the pizzeria every day after school and started working there unofficially as the late-night cleaner. Tony showed me how to clean up the pizzeria properly. I couldn't work behind the counter yet because I was underage, but I would come in after school just to hang out, fold pizza boxes, and run local errands for Tony. I would also make runs with Tony to the wholesale store Jetro's to pick up supplies. Tony showed me how to shop for the business, including how to pick vegetables, meats, tomato sauces, and how to buy the right mozzarella—always whole milk mozzarella cheese, not part-skim. Sorrento and Polly-O were top of the line.

My daily routine became dropping my sister off at the social club with her sitters, dropping off my bookbag at our apartment, and doing my homework before going to the pizzeria. Everything was within a six-block radius from our apartment. I would be in and out of the pizzeria, running errands, folding pizza boxes, until it was time to clean at 9 P.M.

My mom didn't care that I was out late on school nights, as long as I was doing something productive and making money. I had all the pizza I could eat whenever I wanted. My mom was busy with Shailin, who was seven years old, and they were always at the social club while my mom cut hair and played dominoes after work. I'd get home around 11 P.M. and be up in time for school the next day.

The first year and a half, Tony's Pizza shop was a success. The pizza and the food were delicious, and we were busy. Tony's whole family chipped in. Tony's family were all physically on the short side. They were all around five feet tall, except Paulie, who was the oldest brother and the anomaly in the family; he stood at 5'11". Bobby, 5'3", would help with deliveries most nights after he got out of his job as a patient escort in St. Francis Hospital. His mom, Gia, was a retired stay-at-home parent and school lunch attendant. Gia was what you would call a traditional Italian American mother. She had white hair and glasses, a button nose, and could pass for Mrs. Santa Claus. She was a recent breast cancer survivor as well and helped Tony in the kitchen all the time. Tony was a momma's boy. When Gia wasn't helping, she was sitting at her table making sure her son didn't need anything and watching her soap operas—*Days of Our Lives* and *General Hospital*.

Tony's sisters, Donna, and Marie would chip in at the pizzeria in the kitchen and counter. Donna was the oldest sibling. They would alternate and come in during the dinner rush to help answer the phone, cook, and prep. Donna had a full-time job as a nurse at the Jersey City Medical Center, the hospital I was born in. Tony's brother Paulie didn't do much as far as helping. He struggled with addiction like my brother Eddie and had been recently fired from the Welfare Department. He just hung around in his black suit all the time.

Saturday mornings at the pizzeria were prep day and my busiest day of work. I'd be at the pizza shop by 9 A.M. and usually worked with either Marie, Donna, or Gia on the weekly food prep in the kitchen where I wouldn't be seen. Tony would open and he and Bobby would shop for supplies.

Tony's family really embraced me, as I did them. They all treated me like family—like I was one of their own. They'd praise me for being a hard worker and having a good head on my shoulders. They were always encouraging me to stay off the streets. I enjoyed working. It kept me from dwelling on our home situation, off the streets and taught me valuable skills. It allowed me to contribute to my family's well-being, ensuring we didn't go hungry. Working also allowed me to always have a dollar in my pocket to help my mom and myself.

The Contes taught me all their Italian recipes as well. We would start with the sauces. Gia made the "gravy," as she called it. She showed me how to make sure not to let the onions burn in the olive oil. Then she'd add fatty sausage and let that simmer for a bit. Then came the cans of crushed tomatoes, water, followed by the addition of all the spices: oregano, salt, pepper, sugar, parsley, and garlic.

Donna showed me how to peel, clean, and butterfly the shrimp by removing the vein (aka the "shit tube," as Donna would say). We would dip them in flour, eggs, and seasoned Italian breadcrumbs. We would repeat the same process for the chicken and the eggplant.

After that, it was time to shred. I'd slice the three-pound, four-inch-thick logs of mozzarella into four pieces and shred them on the cheese cutter into a cheese container. I would then wrap it and store it in the fridge, ready to go for the afternoon. Slicing mozzarella cheese every day was a great workout for my arms and chest. Cheese cutting made me strong. I had to use a lot of pressure using my whole arm and shoulder to push the blocks of cheese into the twelve-inch blade to get the right thickness for the mozzarella. If shredded too thin, it would melt and burn faster in the oven. Too thick, and the crust would overcook, and the pie would be too cheesy.

Tony also showed me how to make the dough for the pizza pies using a huge, old-school floor mixer. I'd start by adding slightly warm, room-temperature water to the mixer. Then came the salt, vegetable oil, and yeast. I would break down the stinky yeast with my hand to dissolve it into the warm water. Then pick up a fifty-pound bag of white flour, dump it in the mixing bowl, attach the mixing hook, and let the mixer do its job. I'd closely monitor the dough and add flour or water as necessary until it was smooth. Next, it was time to lift all that dough and plop it on the stainless-steel table. That's where we cut and weighed each piece of dough, about a pound and a quarter. We placed them in a tray, dabbed them up with oil on top, and stocked them airtight in the fridge.

    Chino was what the Conte's called me. I got the nickname when I was eight years old, right after we moved into our apartment on 7th Street. Chino means Chinese in Spanish. My neighbor Madelin gave me the name. She said I resembled a young Bruce Lee and the wrestler Ricky Steamboat because of my bowl haircut and my small, deep eyes. So, the nickname stuck in Jersey City. I was now Chino, not Chuchin. I worked seven days a week making forty dollars a week when I started at Tony's.

    So that was my routine, I would drop off my sister Shailin at her babysitters and go straight to Tony's after school, grab a slice, and hang out waiting for Tony to ask me to do something like fold boxes or load the soda cooler. Then I would check in on my mom and sister at the club or the apartment and bring them food before I had to go back to clean the pizzeria. My night would begin with the dishes. The stainless-steel sink had three compartments with a huge powerful sprayer which worked to rinse off any grease or dried food. All the dirty pots and pans of the day would be stacked up. I cleaned every greasy pot and container there was.

After I was done with the dishes, I would move on to cleaning the floor mixer and cheese grater, carefully wiping it all down, making sure there was no cheese stuck anywhere. Then I worked on the steam table that kept all the sauces, meatballs, water, and sausages fresh and hot. By then, the dinner rush was over, and the pizzeria was quiet enough for me to come to the front and clean the pizza station. Using a square spatula, I would gather up all the flour from the counter and wrap all the pizza toppings in plastic wrap—the pepperoni, mushrooms, onions, meatballs, and sausages—and store them in the fridge. Tony would then turn the oven down to two hundred degrees and close the front door.

Most of the time, Tony and Bobby would leave me alone in the pizzeria and head out for a glass of wine around 10:30 P.M. while I finished cleaning up. I would brush the brick in the oven clean with a metal brush and wipe the steel down, making it shine like a new Cadillac. Then I would go to the pizza counter, clean that, and wrap up any leftovers I might want to take home, like a stromboli or sausage roll. After that, I'd wrap up all the garbage bags and take them out to the back alley, finishing with sweeping and mopping. Mopping was the worst. We had a huge commercial mop, and Tony would make me change the water out twice each time. It was a lot of work, but I was willing and hungry to do it. All the cleaning, scrubbing, and mopping made me strong and taught me discipline, along with the value of an honest day's work.

ADRIAN ALVARADO

Tony was teaching me life lessons, especially when it came to money and business. He had big dreams himself: to have a chain of Tony's Famous Pizzerias. As soon as I started accumulating some cash, Tony took me to a bank on Newark Ave to open a savings account. I remember depositing my first $300. I received a small square paper book with my account balance and balance sheets, and Tony showed me how to balance my bank account and make deposits. I would make deposits every week. I couldn't keep cash at home. But first I would try giving my mother half of my weekly cash, but she wouldn't take it. She just smiled and told me to take care of the things I needed for myself, like clothes for school, and to save. Mom was happy with me simply bringing food home.

Even though she wouldn't take my money, I still wanted to give my mom something special. So, by the time Mother's Day came around, I had saved an extra $350 for a gift for her. Tony and his family would always give me cash for my birthday and Christmas, and I would save it all. One day I asked Tony's sister Marie to take me to her jeweler so I could buy my mom a gold necklace so I wouldn't get scammed. Marie had a lot of gold chains and jewelry and had a place she always went to for her gold so I was confident I would get the best quality for my money if she went with me. She took me to the jewelry district in New York. Marie helped me pick out a 14k gold linked chain with a gold emblem spelling the word "Mom" encrusted with small diamonds.

I was working every day at the pizzeria, so on Mother's Day, I asked her to stop by so I could give her the gift. Mom entered dressed in a black dress and her make up on like always. They were having a Mother's Day dinner and dancing at the social club. I reached into my pocket and handed her the small box with the chain. When she opened it, she was speechless, staring at it for a moment with a proud smile. She took the necklace out of the box and dipped the gold emblem with the word "mom" into a pizza pie just over the counter. I was stunned! I had just spent $350 on this chain, and it was made of gold and diamonds! I naturally exclaimed, "Ma, what are you doing?" She smiled and replied, "This came from making pizza, so I'm honoring the pizza." She put the emblem in her mouth and sucked out the sauce and cheese. Then she handed me the necklace and I placed it around her neck. It looked beautiful around her neck. She looked beautiful.

Tony was always preaching, "You gotta work hard and save your money in this world, Chino. A lot of these kids in this neighborhood don't want to work. They just want to hang out on the corner selling drugs. Making babies. Collecting welfare checks."

Tony was right. There was still an actual war on drugs going on in America in the 1980s as well as a teen pregnancy epidemic, and it invaded our neighborhoods, our families, and friends. Tony's brother Paulie, my brother, and a lot of the guys in the neighborhood I knew were losing battles in this drug war. Tony, a devout Catholic, claimed he'd never smoked a cigarette or touched any drugs in his life, and I believed him. It pained and angered him to see his own brother struggle. Tony was uptight and reserved about many things and with people. He had a habit of not revealing his true self, always playing a role with strangers. Though he never touched drugs, Tony enjoyed his wine and Dewars and water.

    During the summer, I would really take my time cleaning the pizza shop. I'd get into my zone, playing Big Daddy Kane's "Smooth Operator," and focus on cleaning the pizza station, wiping down and cleaning everything—the oven, fridges, counters, mirrors, and arcades. Tony gave in a brought in a couple of arcades to make extra money. We always had the newest ones like Street Fighter and Tony would let me take as many quarters as I wanted to play. So, I would have my fill a become one of the best players around. A lot of the neighborhood kids would come challenge me at the pizzeria. I would make Tony extra money while I waited to go to work after school from winning all the time.

    Once I finished cleaning and playing, I would call Tony, and he would pick me up and drop me off at my apartment. Tony wasn't always on time, though, especially on weekends. He would stay at the bar till about midnight or so then finally pick me up. Sometimes I would get the itch and want to hang out as well, like any normal kid. I could hear all the kids hanging outside on the block while I worked and cleaned, but Tony would always advise against it. "Nothing good happens at night around here, Chino. You're not missing anything. Stay out of trouble and in the pizzeria." he would say. I didn't mind at first because he was right. None of the kids I used to hang out with were doing well. Some of my boys were already getting high and smoking. One of my eighth-grade classmates was about to have a baby with his thirteen-year-old girlfriend. So, I listened to Tony and stayed inside. I would turn on the TV, watch Arsenio Hall, play arcades, and do pushups while I waited for Tony.

I was doing well, working, and going to school. But the honeymoon would soon end. Tony's Famous Pizza started running into problems. The seeds of trouble were beginning to surface. Patsy, from 3 Boys, was trying to make good on his promise to Tony and take the shirt off his back. His goal was to push Tony out of business. The newly remodeled 3 Boys Pizza was re-opening next door, and the fact that two pizzerias were next to each other was odd. The neighborhood and the block were beginning to split. Tony had made enemies, and rumors began to spread. Rumors about Tony's personal life and the nature of our relationship. I didn't know it yet, but our lives were about to take a turn.

ADRIAN ALVARADO

CHAPTER 13

IDENTITY

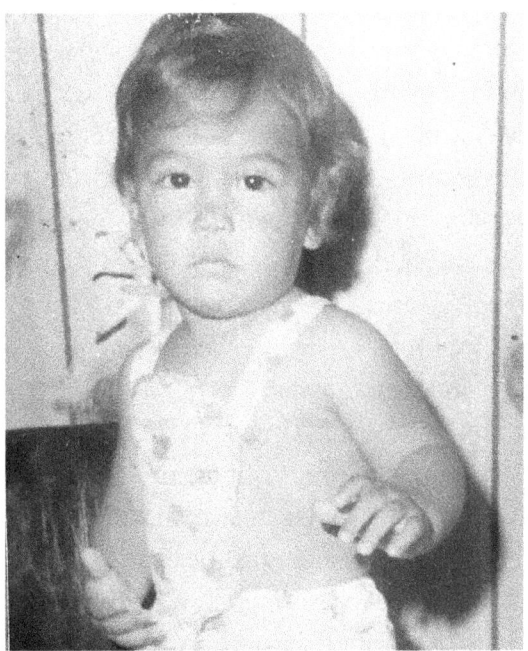

Me, 1 year old-Salinas, Puerto Rico 1977.

I was first told I wasn't a "real American" at Tony's Pizzeria. I was thirteen, hanging out in between the dinner rush playing Street Fighter and singing a song by Rick Derringer called "I Am a Real American." It featured everyone's favorite wrestler at the time, Hulk Hogan playing an electric guitar in the video. I was belting out the chorus:

"I am a real American. Fight for the rights of every man."

On cue, our pizza delivery guy walked in: Tony's cousin Vinny. Vinny, 18 years old, 6'1" with a crooked mouth, was a dead ringer for Sylvester Stallone. When he heard me singing, he teased me and casually said, "You're not a real American, Chino. You're a Puerto Rican." He laughed. I didn't.

What does he mean? I thought to myself. *I was born here. I pledged allegiance to the flag every morning in school. What does he mean I'm not a "real" American?* His comment got me thinking. As I grew older and began to understand the dynamics of race in America, I realized there was some truth to his statement. In school, we were taught about the Pilgrims and the Native Americans of North America. How the French hated the English, the Spanish hated the English, and how they all hated each other but still did business and colonized. The school's curriculum focused on teaching us about George Washington's rotten teeth and the Boston Tea Party, where a bunch of Bostonians dressed as Native Americans, dumped tea into the Boston Harbor in protest and sparking a revolution. We learned of world wars and the civil rights movement. But school didn't teach me about my people and where I came from.

In my seventh-grade history class I recall our teacher Mr. Smith, a black man, was giving his lesson about Dr. Martin Luther King Jr. and the Civil Rights Movement. I raised my hand and asked him, "Mr. Smith, were there any Puerto Ricans during the Civil Rights Movement?" He shook his head and said, "Not many." His response felt incomplete and unsatisfying. It dawned on me that Mr. Smith didn't know our history; he only knew his. The history he was told to teach was what was printed in the Hudson County Board of Education's curriculum. His inadequate answer to my question, combined with Vinny's comment about me not being a "real" American, opened my eyes and woke me up to see how we were looked upon in this country—how I was perceived as a Puerto Rican born in America. Those two seemingly innocuous moments with Vinny and Mr. Smith began my quest for self-discovery. I began to research and learn on my own through encyclopedias. Eventually, I used the internet to learn more about myself and my people.

The Spanish conquistadores were mentioned only briefly in my American education. They first came with that Italian mariner Christopher Columbus on the ships La Niña, La Pinta, and La Santa María, which landed on my ancestral home in 1492. The Spanish ruled the world at one point. Their reach stretched from the Philippines across the globe into the Caribbean.

I kept digging into my culture and background for information and eventually found the first known Alvarado to land in the Antilles Islands of Santo Domingo, Cuba, and Puerto Rico. I was shocked and surprised when I first saw my last name in the encyclopedia. My name was part of history. There he was all along, the Spanish conquistador Pedro de Alvarado. Born in Badajoz, Spain, in 1485, Alvarado was an elite and cruel fighter who later became the second in command to the most famous Spanish conquistador ever, Hernán Cortés, in overthrowing the Aztec Empire. I'm not claiming to be a descendant of Pedro de Alvarado but seeing my last name on paper and having a historical connection was good enough for me. Good or bad, like my dad, Pedro de Alvarado was a man of action. Christopher Minster, Ph.D., a professor at La Universidad de Quito in Ecuador, wrote of Alvarado:

> "In about 1510, he went to the New World with several brothers and an uncle. They soon found work as soldiers in the various expeditions of conquest that originated on Hispaniola (Dominican Republic), including the brutal conquest of Cuba, the Aztecs in Central Mexico in 1519, and Alvarado led the Conquest of the Maya in 1523. Alvarado was blond and fair, with blue eyes and pale skin that fascinated the natives of the New World. He was considered affable by his fellow Spaniards and the other conquistadores trusted him. Referred to as 'Tonatiuh' or 'Sun God' by the Aztecs because of his blonde hair and white skin, Alvarado was violent, cruel, and ruthless, even for a conquistador for whom such traits were practically a given. All the

conquistadores were ruthless, cruel, and bloodthirsty, but Pedro de Alvarado was in a class by himself. He had no legitimate children but did father several illegitimate ones."

Pedro de Alvarado and his conquistador buddies set a precedent in the Caribbean that would be followed by many Puerto Rican men. I believe those conquistadores began the tradition of irresponsible dads on the island. The first generation of mixed Spanish and Arawak born in Puerto Rico and the Americas had no fathers. These were sons of conquistadors who pillaged, enslaved, killed the men, raped the women, and left a whole generation of kids without fathers, just like Pedro de Alvarado himself.

Growing up without a father was commonplace in my neighborhood. Many of my friends were in the same predicament as me. If our dads weren't dead, in jail, or strung out on drugs, they were conquering the modern world of women, racetracks, and casinos. It's right there in the history books, in both Spanish and English. This is why I believe many of us Puerto Ricans still grow up fatherless—it's an ingrained generational trauma. The legacy of the Spanish conquistadores still lives on in the actions of many of their descendants, including my grandfather and father. I knew then it was up to me to change the cycle in my family, to flip my script, to build a solid family foundation for my future wife and kids.

ADRIAN ALVARADO

Growing up, I was always curious about my background and what it meant to be Puerto Rican. Nobody had an answer for me. Dad wasn't there to teach me, and my mom was busy trying to survive. I knew there was more to us than dysfunction, rice, beans, and salsa music. I learned that through continuous exploration, you uncover profound truths. Truths we were not taught in my classroom, like discovering that one of the best players in Major League Baseball history, Puerto Rican Hall of Famer Roberto Clemente, played an integral role in continuing the Civil Rights Movement after Dr. Martin Luther King Jr.'s assassination through his constant service to others. Dr. King was Clemente's hero. So much so that he visited Clemente on his farm in Carolina, Puerto Rico. In 1968, Clemente also spoke up for his teammates and other Black players when they prompted Major League Baseball to pause Opening Day until after Dr. Martin Luther King's funeral. Roberto Clemente would tragically lose his life on a relief mission to deliver supplies to earthquake victims in Nicaragua. His cargo plane crashed into the ocean off the coast of San Juan shortly after takeoff. He was 38. (Ortiz)

Reflecting on my early education and the origins of our history with the conquistadores, it frustrates me to acknowledge their deplorable actions. At the time, I yearned to embrace a sense of pride in my Spanish heritage, hoping to feel connected to their history. Instead, I found myself feeling like a mutt while they possessed royalty, wealth, and tradition. I couldn't comprehend why. Eventually, life teaches you about human behavior, and if you pay attention to history, you come to understand that it is all part of the process of dividing and conquering. Puerto Rico and its people have endured centuries of exploitation, a reality that continues to resonate even today.

Most folks can easily identify with their genetic blueprint. They can say, I am Irish. I am German. I am Greek. I am Swedish. Me, I am Puerto Rican, and I knew our DNA was a little more complex. So, as soon as our gene technology advanced and became accessible, I couldn't resist. Yes, I gave up my spit and DNA to the elite dark shadow government so they can officially do whatever they want with it. I wanted a sense of my European, African and native heritage. The rumor growing up was that much of the population in Puerto Rico had a mix of African, Taino Indigenous, and Spanish blood, with dashes of the rest of the world mixed in but how much of that was true and what other nations could be part of my make up?

My DNA results confirmed that I am a blend of various cultures and ancestries, a living testament to the island's rich and complex history. The mix of Taino/Arawak, African and European roots isn't just a concept; it's imbedded in my DNA. This intricate combination shapes our identity, our traditions and our shared sense of belonging. As I prepare to reveal the results of my DNA test, I feel a deep connection to this diverse heritage. Knowing that my story is part of a larger tapestry that defines what it means to be Puerto Rican.

Officially, I am:

27% Iberian Peninsula (Spain/Portugal)
18% Indigenous Puerto Rico
14% Cameroon, Congo, Western Bantu Peoples
9% Wales
6% Mali
6% Basque
6% England & Northern Europe
3% Benin & Togo
3% Northern Africa
3% Jewish
2% Senegal
1% Nigerian
1% Indigenous Americas – Mexico
1% Scotland.

CHAPTER 14

HARSH TRUTHS

Mom and me at my eighth-grade graduation, June 1990.

It was 1990. Nelson Mandela was released from prison in South Africa after twenty-seven years and became the leader of the ANC after forty-six years of apartheid. Francis Ford Coppola's *The Godfather Part III* almost ruined "The Godfather" legacy, and a white rapper named Vanilla Ice had the summer's hit with "Ice, Ice, Baby."

ADRIAN ALVARADO

My home life was still somehow deteriorating. We finally got a Section 8 assisted apartment on Kent St., uptown. The farther away you went from downtown, the more dangerous the neighborhoods got. Mom was still struggling, and work just seemed to be non-existent. Her energy was changing. At home, she was always in her room and distant, smoking her cigarettes. My sister Shailin was eight, and my big brother was still a handful.

The day of my eighth-grade graduation, my mom and I were standing outside No. 5 school taking pictures after the ceremony. The New Jersey turnpike was our backdrop as we smiled at my disposable Kodak 35-millimeter camera. Mom had on a black dress with white buttons. Her long brunette hair was straight and in a long ponytail. Her makeup was on point, and she was wearing her typical red lipstick. But there was something different about her today. She was moving gingerly. She grabbed her stomach, complained of a little pain, and wanted to rest. She hugged, kissed, and congratulated me. She apologized that she couldn't celebrate the rest of the day with me. I told her it was fine. We really didn't have any plans, anyway.

A few days after my graduation ceremony, my mom admitted herself to the Jersey City Medical Center for same-day surgery. Mom was back home a few days later, and I was back to my summer routine of working at Tony's all day. I wasn't sure what was happening to her, and I'm not sure she did either. A couple of weeks passed filled with hospital visits and more tests. Soon after mom ended up getting admitted to the hospital again. Tony kept me occupied at the pizzeria and eventually I started to stay at the Conte's. My mom and sister weren't home, and my brother Eddie was always in and out. I would be alone sometimes. Tony's sister Donna convinced me to stay with them. The next day, a call came to the pizzeria. Tony answered and handed the phone to me. "It's your Uncle Isidro."

My Uncle Isidro? Really? I thought. *He'd never called the pizzeria before. He'd never even been to the pizzeria.* I grabbed the phone and asked for his blessing as we do our elders as a sign of respect, "Bendición." He gave me his blessing, "Dios te bendiga," (God bless you) and told me we were having a family meeting tonight, and my cousins Sonia and Marcus were going to pick me up shortly. Sonia arrived twenty minutes later, and I got in the car with her and my cousin Marcus. I knew it was serious because Tony never let me go home early.

Sonia, Marcus, and I arrived at my Aunt Rita's apartment, who now lived in the Greenville neighborhood of Jersey City. Everyone was gathered in the living room. Even my grandma Estelle was there—she had flown in from Puerto Rico. The only one missing was my mom. My Uncle Isidro, the youngest and only male, took the lead. Isidro was handsome, with light brown skin sporting short comb back black hair and a mustache. He was always funny and charismatic, but today, he was serious. He pulled no punches and got right to the point, "We got some sad news from the doctor. Nena has Stage Four stomach cancer. They said she's got less than a year to live."

His voice suddenly became an echo in my head. What he was saying bounced in my cranium like a pinball. *What? Cancer? My mom? She's going to die?* His words resonated through my body like a gut punch. I instinctively grabbed my own stomach and began to cry. The room was tense and silent. All I could hear were my own cries of despair and my Uncle Isidro's voice in the distance. I'd never cried like that before. It felt different inside. It was a deep vibration in my gut that felt like a tornado twisting inside me. My Grandma Estelle, next to me, was consoling me. *This can't be happening*, I thought to myself. *Not to my mom. Not to me.*

The mood in the room suddenly shifted. The attention was still focused on me. My uncle took the lead again and laid it all out. There was something else. Uncle Isidro began to express concerns about my job at the pizzeria. They'd heard rumors about Tony.

He continued, "We heard a few things about Tony. We heard he is gay. Is something going on with you two? Has he tried anything with you? If so, you cannot work there anymore, and I will go down there and talk to him."

I couldn't deny it. There was a rumor, and it was spreading fast. Rumors about Tony and me. I had literally just started hearing about it right before my family brought it up. "What? No! Absolutely not! None of that is true," I said. "I don't know why people are saying that about me. I just work there. I know I spend a lot of time there but that's my job. I have nowhere else to go." I was pissed that this was happening and that people I didn't even know were saying those things about me. I had a girlfriend at the time, Angelica. Tony never approved of her and kept warning me about her. Angelica and I didn't see each other much because of work, but we did have our little adventures together, making out whenever we had a moment. I'd always been into girls. But that's not the point. I said to my family, "No matter what happens, I can handle myself. If anything, Tony and his family have been helping and supporting me. I don't know what he does in his personal life after work, and I don't care. He's always working, seven days a week, building his business."

 My Uncle Isidro looked at me and told me, "If it's true, you need to eliminate yourself from that environment. Or I will." I nodded my head, crying. I told them that they could speak to Tony's family if they wanted to, including his mom and his sisters.

 I was already staying with the Contes, which didn't help the rumors, but Tony and his family were looking out for me. My uncle looked me in the eyes, and he agreed. I bowed my head. I was hurting and still trying to grasp the news about my mother. *Now this.*

 Everything in my world was changing, again. My mind was racing. I was confused. I was angry. My heart was pounding. I kept asking myself if this was really happening. It felt surreal, like an out-of-body experience.

My feet and hands were tingling. A knot constantly formed in my throat whenever I thought of my mom and my future without her.

Shortly after the family meeting, my cousin Sonia drove me back to Tony's. I remember walking into the pizzeria and seeing the look of sadness on Tony and his family's faces. They already knew. They all gave me a big hug and told me to stay strong. I was still emotional and went into the bathroom to chill out and try to decompress from the gut punch that had hit me that night. I just remember sitting in the bathroom with my hands in my face crying. I was thinking of my mom, and my emotions ranged from sadness to rage. I wanted to wreck the bathroom and punch the walls.

The Contes were more aware of my mother's situation than my own family or I was. Tony's sister Donna was the head nurse at the Jersey City Medical Center, where my mom had been admitted. As the head nurse in the E.R., Donna had access to medical information about my mother's diagnosis. Tony and his sister Donna spoke to my aunts and uncle that night about how they would take me in and look after me while my family sorted out my mom's situation. They assured my family that the rumors were not true. That I was safe. The rumors were coming from a specific source on the block, and we all knew who they were.

Tony and I would eventually face these thugs and personally deal with this later with fists and blood. Till then, I had to worry about my mom and my living situation. My stepdad Luis took over caring for my little sister Shailin immediately after my mom was admitted to the hospital, so she was taken care of. My Aunt Rita's apartment was full of family from Puerto Rico so there was no room for me there. I was already staying with the Contes. At that point, I was familiar with the Contes and had already spent a few holidays with them. I already felt like I was part of Tony's family, and they treated me as such.

My dad and Zuly had separated, which eliminated that option, otherwise I would have stayed with them. My family was reluctant, but I assured them I was safe and that I could handle myself. They finally agreed to let me stay with the Contes. Tony's mom Gia owned the building right around the corner from the pizzeria, on 3rd Street. You could throw a rock from Tony's Pizzeria and hit the building. Tony, his mom, and all his siblings lived in the apartment building. Tony's dad, Tony Conte Sr. left the building to them when he passed away. His brother Bobby lived on the top floor with his wife and new son Bobby Jr. His sister Donna and her new husband lived on the bottom floor. Marie, Paulie, and Tony all lived together in the second-floor apartment with their mom, Gia. It was a three-bedroom railroad apartment with plenty of space.

It was the summer, and I was supposed to be getting ready for high school. Aside from work, I wanted to go to football camp and spring baseball tryouts. The previous fall I had played quarterback for the tackle football for the city's recreational youth league. Tony had even helped me set up an old car tire on a tree behind his mom's building. I would go there right after school, do one hundred pushups, and throw the football through the middle of the tire as target practice for about a half hour before I had to go to work.

Our routine didn't change much. After we closed the pizza shop, Tony would go out for wine like usual. Now, instead of me waiting for him to pick me up, after I was done cleaning, I would walk around the corner to his mom's apartment and crash on the couch.

CHAPTER 15

A MOTHER'S PAIN

Nilda Rivera at age 19.

It was 1990, the middle of summer, and my new routine consisted of visiting my mom during the day at the hospital whenever I could and going to work at Tony's. Mom was beginning to fight her battle with cancer. I would bring her balloons and chocolates before work. Just because the doctor said so, it didn't mean it was final—or at least, that's what I would tell myself. I was praying for a miracle. We all were. I spent my days trying to distract myself from my situation at the pizzeria, but things were different. I started having panic attacks and crying episodes when I thought about my mom dying. I'd randomly run to the bathroom in the pizzeria and lock myself inside. The bathroom was the only place I could be by myself. Where I could let my guard down, escape, cry, agonize, think, and cry some more. Tony and his family would stand by the door and console me while I wept. I'd often here them behind the door saying things like, "We're here for you, Chino.' "Stay strong." "We love you."

Tony Conte and his family were vital during this period of my life. Tony did everything he could to keep my mood positive. Not only did he set up the tire for my football practice, but he also set up a little gym in the basement of his mom's building. He already had a bench and some weights; I enjoyed working out and boxing, so he let me set up a punching bag and a speed bag as well.

Summer was ending and I knew I wasn't going to play football that season. I had missed football camp, and my mind was just not in it. I was in a fog. It was hard not to think of my mother. It was hard to think of life without her in it. A lot of unknowns were swirling in my thoughts. A lot of doubt and self-pity. The "Why me?". It just didn't make sense in my mind. It still doesn't.

Another day goes by and as usual, after closing time, Tony would go drinking his wine and I would go down to the basement and do my best to forget about my life situation by drowning out my confused thoughts with sports radio. I'd hear John Sterling call the Yankee game hoping to hear Don Mattingly hit one out of the park. I'd hit the heavy bag and bench press, do curls and shoulders, anything to keep myself busy. Working out and the Yankees helped. A little.

At first, mom was doing well. She was still alert and going through treatment. But then she quickly took a turn for the worst and began deteriorating fast. A few weeks after getting the news she was terminal, she was transferred to Manhattan's top Cancer Hospital, Sloan Kettering. She was on welfare and on Medicaid. This was only possible because of Tony's sister Donna. Donna filed the right paperwork and pulled the right strings to get my mother the best care possible. This also meant that my mom was farther away from me. Because of the distance, I could only visit my mom on Saturday mornings before work. Her new hospital was on 53rd St and 1st Ave. in the Upper East side neighborhood of Manhattan. I would take the Path Train on Grove Street to the city and hop on the 6 train on 33rd Street by myself. My Grandma Estelle was always in the room, taking care of her and praying the Rosary prayer. I would stop by to drop off flowers. My mom would save face and act like she was fine, but she wasn't. I knew she was in pain. Her face was unnaturally pale and her eye sockets deep and dark. I wouldn't stay long because it was too gut wrenching to see her in her pain and I felt helpless not be able to help her.

ADRIAN ALVARADO

September came fast and I started my first year at Ferris High School while my mom was still in the hospital fighting the good fight. I was still in the same fog. In school I just went through the motions of learning how to go from class to class and then work after school. A few weeks later I ran into my cousin Marcus in the locker room after gym class. Marcus was a sophomore. He sat next to me as we changed out of our gym clothes and quietly whispered, "Yo cuz, your mom took a turn for the worse. You need to go see her soon, bro. If you want, we can go together tomorrow—Saturday."

It had been a week or so since my last visit. I'd gotten caught up with classes and freshman orientation. The last time I'd visited her was so emotional and hard. I guess I kept myself busy to avoid feeling the pain. The reality that she was slowly slipping away was too much to bear.

Marcus and I took the train to the city the next morning. We got off the 6 train, and I stopped at the corner kiosk as usual to buy her some flowers. We walked through the entrance and checked in at the front desk. Then we made our way up the elevator. When the elevator doors opened, we immediately heard the screams and cries of someone in pain. *Shit! I recognize that voice. That's my mom!*

We rushed into her room, opened the door, and found my mom in excruciating pain. Her stomach was so swollen she looked like she was nine months pregnant and going into labor. The cancer in her stomach was causing constipation, and she was about to explode. I made eye contact and asked her what she needed, and she told me, "Llama la enfermera! Mas medicina!" (Call the nurse! More medicine!).

Marcus and I rushed to the nurse's station and told them that my mom was in pain, and she needed help. The nurse didn't even look at us. Instead, she kept her eyes on her chart, and said, "I'm sorry, but we just gave her some meds a little while ago. We can't keep giving it to her whenever she wants it." I pleaded, "But she's in pain!" The nurse finally looked at me, and I guess she must have taken pity on a teary fourteen-year-old kid not wanting to see his mother suffering because she agreed to check on her and give her medication. Immediately after they injected the medication into her I.V., her bowels released, and she stopped screaming. I felt relief that she was free of pain, but I was also angry that my mother was now lying in her hospital bed riddled with cancer and soiled in her own feces. I was angry about the fact that I'd found my mom screaming in pain. What would have happened if I hadn't shown up? Were they prepared to ignore her and let her suffer and slowly die in agony?

Mom laid her head back and drifted into a sleep and we stepped out as the nurses began to clean her. My cousin and I decided to leave. We got in the elevator, stood there, and rode it silently. Both of us stared at the elevator door trying to make sense of what we'd just seen. I could feel him looking at me from the corner of his eye, not knowing what to say or how to comfort me.

He finally laid his hand on my shoulder as the doors opened. I was barely holding it together.

A few days later, I was told by my Aunt Rita to bring my little sister to see Mom, at Mom's request. Shailin had just turned nine years old. On our way to the hospital, I reiterated to Shailin that mommy was sick, and she might not be feeling well. I was afraid we might find her in pain like the last time I'd visited. To our surprise, my mom was standing when we entered the room. Grandma Estelle was there helping her eat lunch. I couldn't believe my eyes. Mom had been bedridden for months. How could she be standing up and looking more alert than ever? For a moment I felt hopeful to see her standing up on her own. No. I quickly realized that she was using all the energy she had left in her so she could get up from the bed and hug her little girl one last time. She didn't want Shailin's last memory of her to be in pain or lying on a hospital bed. I understand that now.

I saw her as she kissed and stroked Shailin's hair, kissing her face, tears slowly rolling down her cheeks. Shailin was oblivious to what was really happening. She hadn't seen mom the whole summer, and now this was the last time she would ever see her mother. Nena just stared at her baby girl. Probably taking in as much as much of her as she could while she pretended to eat. As much as mom tried, it was obvious that she could no longer eat, stand, or sit up on her own. So, my grandma and I helped her back to bed. She hugged and kissed Shailin again and told her, "Te quiero para siempre." (I love you forever). She then turned to me and asked me to take care of Shailin, and to treat my grandma like I treated her. I nodded my head yes. Knowing inside me these were her last wishes.

We stepped out to the hall and said goodbye to our Grandma Estelle. I grabbed my sister by the hand and took her away. On the elevator, my sister had such a confused, innocent look on her face. She mentioned that mommy looked different. Thats probably why Shailin was so taken aback when she saw mom. She didn't recognize her as the mom she knew. I told her that mommy was sick, but not to worry because daddy and I were going to help take care of her now. She smiled excitedly and squeezed my hand.

The news from the doctors was that my mom could pass any day now. The very next day, I was back on the 6 train, heading uptown to the hospital again. This time, I was alone. I had turned a new leaf. This was the day I would become a man. I was determined to be strong for mom as I went to say my final goodbye.

The reality that my mom was never going to be in my life again was quickly becoming truth. I sat on the 6 train watching the busy New Yorkers rush in and out of the sliding doors. Their faces were oblivious to my grief, my struggle, my pain. I wondered if any of them were going through what I was going through, or something similar. We all will at some point. You just always wish you had more time. In hindsight, despite the difficulty of the situation I was fortunate. Few of us get to say goodbye to loved ones right before they pass on.

I kept thinking: *Is this really happening to me? Why is this happening to me? How did we get to this point?* The train ride felt surreal. All these people were going to different moments in their lives. Me too - to say goodbye to my mother for the last time. Nothing made sense. I questioned God in my heart and thought. *I never really had a father, now you're taking my mother! Why?*

I got off the train and as usual grabbed some flowers on the corner before I headed up to the room. My lips began to quiver, and my stomach was filled with butterflies as I rode the elevator up to my mom's floor. So much for being strong. I wasn't sure what I was walking into. I closed my eyes and kept telling myself, *calm down, breathe, I can do this,* trying to control my emotions and prepare myself for the unknown. I opened my eyes, stepped off the elevator, and as I walked towards mom's room, I saw grandma sitting right outside the room holding her rosary beads. Grandma Estelle's face had a look of exhaustion. She was a devoted Catholic and prayed the rosary in mom's room all day and night every day, like clockwork since her arrival from Aibonito. I greeted her with a hug and a kiss, and she told me to go into the room. Mom was in her bed now with medical equipment and machines all around her. She was connected to I.V.s, a morphine drip and attached to a machine that was breathing for her. Her chest unnaturally went up and down. Her breathing felt forced.

Scientists say that when you're dying the last sense you lose is your hearing. Mom had stopped talking right after Shailin and I visited. She truly was harnessing all the strength she had left in her for her final moment with her daughter and me and broke down right after. Although she was in this state, I felt like there was a chance she could still hear me. I held her hand in mine and leaned in, making sure I spoke clearly into her ear. "Mommy. I love you. I'm going to be alright. I'm going to be successful, and I'm always going to be there for Shailin. I'm going to be strong for the family and you don't have to worry about us anymore."

As I spoke, I could see tears begin to roll down her cheeks. It gave me a sense of peace. *It's true*, I thought to myself, she can still hear me. I wiped her tears away and mine, and I kissed her on the forehead. Goodbye.

To this day, it was the hardest thing I've ever had to do. In that moment I knew I would lose her. I would be on my own. I took a deep breath and walked slowly towards the door, looking back at her, knowing this would likely be the last time I saw my mom alive. My grandma met me at the door. Her own eyes were full of tears. I hugged her and told her that I was going to be ok. She began to cry and told me she knew. I looked back again before walking out.

ADRIAN ALVARADO

CHAPTER 16

A BROTHER'S KEEPER

Edwardo Alvarado

Despite my big brother Eddie having his troubles, he had a knack for being there at the most important times in my life. I passionately believe that if my brother wasn't home the night my stepfather Luis pulled a knife out on my mom, none of us would be here. But he was, and now, he showed up for me again, just in time. Like a guardian angel.

It was Friday, October 5, 1990. My mother was still unresponsive. The machines attached to her had become her and my family was gathering at the hospital waiting for the imminent moment. When I got to the hospital, the room was filled with family. Grandma Estelle, Aunt Rita, and all my relatives were praying the rosary. It was a constant hum in my mother's hospital room. Everyone was keeping in rhythm, and my grandma was the prayer warrior leading the meditation. I stood in silence with my eyes fixed on Mom and the machines pumping her oxygen: breathing in, pause, out, up, pause down.

    I couldn't take it anymore. It was all too overwhelming, and I felt an anxiety attack coming on. I made my way out of the room towards the waiting room at the end of the hall seeking relief, only to be turned around by an agonizing shriek. My Aunt Luisa came running down the hall screaming and weeping: "Se murió! Se murió!" ("She died! She died!").

    I rushed back to the room but was cut off by Aunt Dhalia trying to protect me from what was inside. She tried to console me, but I ran past her. Family members were spilling out of the room, crying, and sobbing. I entered the room and saw my mother. Her chest was no longer pumping. Her mouth was open, and her eyes were staring up toward the heavens. It was as if her soul had been wrestling a long time to get out of her body and when the moment finally came, it did so in haste. Finally free to fulfill her next destiny. Everything around me stopped. I couldn't see or hear anyone around me. I stood next to her bed holding her hand. Time stood still. Only my mom and I existed at that moment. I was brought back by the nurse who'd come to close my mom's eyes and place a towel under her chin to keep her mouth closed. She began to turn off all the machines that were keeping mom alive. I saw my Uncle Isidro at the foot of her bed holding her feet with his head down, sobbing. He took it the hardest out of all the siblings. This was his big sister. This was it. It happened. My mom was gone. Nilda (Nena) Rivera passed away at 7:40 P.M. on October 5, 1990. She was forty-three.

I was transfixed on my mom's body. I wasn't crying. I just stood there like a ghost, invisible, in shock. Wanting to take it all in before they took her away. Family members began trying to take me out of the room as they sobbed. I wasn't ready to leave her. I wanted to be left alone and see her at peace. I just stared at her. My Grandma Estelle was crying on the other side of the bed. Hearing her suffering suddenly gave me a rush of anger, and I ran out of the room.

I jetted down the hallway enraged. I rushed to the bathroom and kicked open the door. I wanted to smash everything in that bathroom. Just then, Eddie burst through the door behind me. He grabbed me hard and said, "Calm down, Adrian. It's over. Mommy is in a better place now. She's not suffering anymore." He smiled and hugged me.

Eddie was there to protect and comfort me. His words covered me like a soothing blanket, and I suddenly felt a sense of calm. He was right. Mom wasn't suffering anymore. After months of being bedridden with the realization that her time here on earth was limited, being poked, tested, medicated, being in pain, suffering, watching her family suffer, and dealing with the dreadful reality of leaving her kids behind, Mom was finally able to rest in peace. She was free of cancer. She was free to be with God, her ancestors and to continue to be able to watch over us from a different dimension.

Later that night, everyone gathered at my Aunt Rita's apartment where the sorrow continued. Throughout my mom's illness, my grandma Estelle kept it together for the family. Yes, she cried at the hospital with all of us, but once at my Aunt Rita's house, knowing it was the end, she finally allowed herself to let go. As soon as we got to the apartment, my grandma fell to the floor, grabbing at her heart in agony. I had never heard such a painful scream come out of a person before. "Why? Why did you take my daughter? She was the good one," she wailed in Spanish.

In the kitchen nearby, I could hear the grumblings of the now oldest in the family, my Aunt Rita, snarling under her breath, "What, and I'm the bad one?" as she smoked her cigarette. Hearing my grandmother wail for her daughter and watching everyone trying to console her was too much for me. I couldn't bear my sadness along with everyone else's. I got up and made my way to the only private bedroom in the apartment in the hopes of some peace and quiet. The TV was on, but no one was there. I was relieved to be alone and closed the door behind me. I sat on the bed and took a moment. For the first time, I was alone with my thoughts, and I felt an instant connection to Mom's spirit. I began talking to her. Memories of her life consumed me. They were flashing across my mind like slides. An image of her face appeared. She was smiling. I immediately started to pray. I was praying that she was okay. That she was truly in a better place and had made it across to her next spiritual chapter. I asked her to give me a sign, any sign, so that my heart and soul could be at peace. Suddenly, out of nowhere, the TV shut off. No joke. I freaked out and looked around. I checked the plug to make sure it was plugged in. It was. Maybe I was just being a hopeful superstitious fourteen-year-old, but I took it as the sign I had asked for. She was okay and she was smiling and at peace. I felt an overwhelming sense of calm. I laid my head down on the pillow and fell into a deep sleep.

    I woke up to the voices of my brother Eddie and a nasally voice talking in Spanish next to me. It was my father, Felix. There he was. Grandma Coca's Flaco. Here in my time of need. He gave me a big smile and said, "Adrian, Estás bien?" ("Adrian, are you okay?") I nodded yes. Then, he said, "Let's go and get something to eat," in his thick Puerto Rican accent.

    Felix, Eddie, and I ended up at The Flamingo Diner in Downtown Jersey City. It was on the corner of Green and Montgomery St. by Exchange Place. Everybody in the city went to The Flamingo. I had been there many times with Tony and his brothers. We sat in a booth, and

I ordered my favorite—a BLT with mayo on white toast. This was my first time ever eating out with my dad and brother. I really don't remember much of the conversation, but what I do remember is a lot of laughing. It seemed that whenever my dad and brother got together, it was a razz fest on each other. Eddie, the constant joker, always had something to poke fun at. This time it was my dad's big head. Eddie jokingly said, "What did Nena ever see in you?" We all laughed. Dad then asked me if I wanted to move in with him. I shrugged my shoulders in reply. I told him that I wasn't sure what I was going to do. That I needed time.

    I appreciated that my dad wanted to be there for me, but I knew his living situation wasn't ideal for me at that moment. He was no longer with Zuly and my little sisters. Zuly left him. Even after having another daughter together Zulisa, they still couldn't work out their situation. If Zuly were in the picture, I would've taken him up on his offer to stay with him. But he was now shacked up with a wild lady named Iris. My dad seemed to be going downhill, and putting myself in the middle of his living situation did not seem like the right thing for me. We finished our meal and headed back to my aunt's apartment.

    The next day was a crisp Fall Day. My family began the preparations for my mom's funeral and her transport back to Puerto Rico. Before she passed, Mom requested she be buried on the island, with her grandparents, in the high mountains of Aibonito where she was born. Even though I was only fourteen, I was incredibly involved in the process. Money was scarce. It seemed like no one in the family had money for the funeral. Luckily, I had saved about $3,000 with Tony's help working at the pizzeria since I was eleven. Tony was good like that and instilled smart money habits in me. "Save your money, Chino!" he would say. "Save your money for a rainy day." This is what he meant by a rainy day.

Even though my mom didn't want a funeral here in the states, La Vieja and El Viejo, the owners of the social club, pleaded with my Grandma Estelle to please have a wake here in Jersey City before we took her back to Puerto Rico. Everyone at the social club wanted a chance to honor her memory and say their goodbyes. My grandma obliged. My Aunt Rita and I went to the Introcaso-Angelo Funeral Home on Brunswick Street in Downtown Jersey City. The mortician walked us around a room full of coffins and showed them to us like he was selling Cadillacs. He showed us designs and the features of each coffin. He opened a dark sky-blue one and inside it had a flock of geese flying in a V-shape pattern. "This one signifies flying home," he told us. It was a nice color and looked amazingly comfortable as a final resting place for my mom. My aunt negotiated the price, and then, a deposit had to be made for the wake. I reached into my pocket and gave my aunt $1,500.

The funeral in Jersey City was packed. I purchased a black suit and composed myself. I had shed all my tears while Mom was suffering; now it was time to gather strength. In the casket my mom looked like her beautiful self again. Her hair was shorter than usual because they had to cut it at the hospital, but her face was pretty and at peace. Everyone who typically attended the Saturday softball games at the park was present, paying their respects. The crowd included her domino partners and hair customers, along with countless others. Seeing all these people there made me realize how many lives my mom had touched. She was genuinely loved by many. My dad was one of the first people to arrive, as well as all members of my mom's family who were in Jersey. Aunt Maritza was also there. She drove all the way from Dayton, Ohio. Maritza asked me then and there if I wanted to live with her. She was open and willing to take me in. I thanked her and requested she let me get back from Puerto Rico first before I made that decision. The evening ended, and it was time to go.

The next day, we took Mom back home to Aibonito, Puerto Rico where the second wake was held. My whole family was there. Even Grandma Coca came from Salinas. It was great to see her. I didn't realize until then how much I'd missed her. We fulfilled my mother's last request and laid her to rest with her grandparents. My brother Eddie and I were the lead pallbearers.

I had big dreams for my mom and me. I was going to make it out of poverty and buy her a house, like I thought any son should. I wanted to see my mom happy by giving her something to be proud of, but it wasn't meant to be. Cancer had its way with her. Her loss left me feeling empty. I realized I would never know her dreams and who she was as a woman. Life didn't give us the opportunity to have those conversations. And now, I knew I never would. It made me angry all over again. I became withdrawn, a loner.

Losing her made me look at the world and everyone in it differently. It left me searching for even more answers about who I was, my heritage, and who we are as collective people in America and as Puerto Ricans. Her death taught me the life lesson that all could be gone in an instant; nothing was guaranteed. It made me question God—His existence and purpose for me. Religious folks would always say that God has a plan. He always takes the good ones because He has a bigger purpose for them in Heaven. I asked God why my mom was taken when I still needed her here. My mom was my entire world, my love, the single most important person in my life, and nobody could give me comfort or a reason. The worst possible thing that could ever happen in my life had just happened. Now what?

ADRIAN ALVARADO

CHAPTER 17

CHOICES

At my mom's funeral. My dad Felix on the left with my sister Zulisha, my brother Eddie, Aunt Maritza, and me on the right. Oct. 1990.

After my mother's funeral, I had to make the choice of who to live with. I had three options: My dad's offer remained open, and the prospect of a new beginning for us sounded tempting. However, I was aware that my dad's lifestyle remained his main priority. Despite his heartfelt intentions, his actions spoke differently. Zuly warned me about his new girl, Iris, and how she was trouble. I believed Zuly. She wasn't just being a jealous ex. I'd met Iris after their split and didn't like her vibe at all. She lived the same lifestyle my dad was living, the hustler's life. She had three sons, and while I didn't know them personally, I was familiar with them all. They walked and talked hard. While working at Tony's, I would see everyone's face in the neighborhood or hear of them. I agreed with Zuly that living with my dad wouldn't be the best option for me. I thanked my dad for his offer but had to turn him down. As it would turn out, this decision was wise because two years later, Iris stabbed my dad in the stomach, almost killing him.

My second choice should've been an easy decision, my Aunt Maritza. Aunt Maritza had traveled a long way to my mother's wake in Jersey City. Her main goal, aside from paying her respects, was to bring me back to Dayton, Ohio after my mom's burial. Maritza was the first of Grandma Coca's children to graduate from college, becoming an electrical engineer. She was highly intelligent, strong, an all-star softball player, and a competitive weightlifter in college. My aunt outlifted most men on leg presses and may still holds the record for batting average at the University of Mayaguez in Puerto Rico. Her athletic abilities awarded her scholarships, but her brains got her ahead. As soon as she graduated, she jumped on the first job offer she got with the United States Department of Defense as a civilian electrical engineer. And just like that, Aunt Maritza went from a tropical paradise to the cold of the Midwest in Dayton, Ohio, working at Wright Brothers Air Force Base. Maritza moved there with her partner Margie and her two daughters, Tammy and Rosie. A true modern family in the 1980s.

Two years prior to my mother's death, I'd spent a summer with them in Dayton. It was the first summer that I wasn't sent to Puerto Rico. I always had a great time with my aunt. But good times and success come with discipline, and my Aunt Maritza had plenty of it. Maritza had a strong personality and was strict. I remember one time during one of my summer visits to Puerto Rico, Aunt Maritza was on break from the university. I was nine years old, and we were all watching TV in the living room. I was snacking on something and chewing loudly with my mouth open, which was the only thing in the world that would make my grandma upset with me. My Grandma Coca was always sweet with me, but she had only two pet peeves that would set her off. One was hitting the plate loudly with your fork as you ate, and the other was chewing with your mouth open. These were big no-no's for grandma. But the only people who would enforce it were my grandma and my Aunt Maritza. So, I'm sitting on the floor, chewing away in front of the TV, when I get a warning from Aunt Maritza: "Cierra la boca." (Close your mouth).

I corrected myself for a second, but a minute later, I started chewing with my mouth open again. Suddenly, Aunt Maritza got up and pinched my lips together with her fingers. She somehow had a sewing needle or toothpick in her hand which she put close to my pinched lips insinuating she would sew my lips shut to keep me from chewing with my mouth open. "You are not a cow or a horse to eat that way!" she said. Well, you can say corporal punishment works sometimes. I was traumatized but from that moment on I've always been aware of how I chew my food. I now cringe whenever I hear someone around me do it. Aunt Maritza was tough, but she was also loving and fun. She would always say to me, "My Prince Chuchin." Then smother me with kisses. She was very affectionate with me like Grandma. During her college breaks, she'd take me everywhere on the island, we'd do excursions like camping on the beach where we'd cook rice, beans, and fried pork in a fire pit built in the sand. We'd make long road trips to visit her friends by the river and make bathroom pit stops on the highway.

Aunt Maritza had no children of her own, so she was the obvious choice for me to live with. It was a no-brainer. She absolutely loved me and would give me a good life. She would make sure I got the best educational opportunities. She was adventurous and loved the outdoors. I could totally see my life with Maritza and her family in Dayton. I would never again have to worry about buying my own sneakers and school clothes. I would never need to help pay bills or buy my own Christmas presents. I could be a normal kid growing up in the Midwest and leave Jersey City behind. Start anew or I could go with the third choice.

My third choice was complicated. During my mother's illness, my sister Shailin was staying with her dad Luis. He finally got his wish and had full custody of Shailin. I'd stopped staying with the Contes, and Eddie and I were now temporarily staying with Aunt Rita. It was already a cramped situation at her apartment. Eddie was only there for a couple of days because he still had his issues, and Rita didn't trust him in her home. She didn't seem to want me living there either. Aunt Rita and I were never chummy. As a kid, I always remember her being distant and cranky. Let's just say we weren't each other's favorite. Sometimes people's personalities just don't mesh well. But I also had somewhat of a theory. My theory was Aunt Rita felt a certain way about me because of my dad and his treatment of my mother. She was not a fan, and I resembled him, which was a constant reminder to her. Aunt Rita and I both knew this wasn't an ideal situation, but we were family. She knew how my dad was living, and she understood that living with him wouldn't be ideal for me. Despite our distance, Aunt Rita stepped up and offered me her home. I would be sharing a room with both my cousins Sonia and Marcus, and sharing a full-sized bed with Marcus, who was now 6'2".

It wasn't an easy decision for me. No matter who I decided to live with, it wouldn't be a perfect situation. But deep in my heart, I already knew on the day of my mother's passing where I was going to stay. I had a promise to keep. I'd promised my mom on her deathbed that I was going to make it no matter what. I also

ADRIAN ALVARADO

promised that I would always look out for my little sister. Shailin and I were close. Despite the dysfunction surrounding us we grew up together. I couldn't leave her. If I went and lived in Dayton, Ohio, God knows when we would see each other again. She needed her big brother to look out for her in those mean streets. I'd just lost my mother, and I couldn't stand the thought of losing my baby sister as well. I had to stay. So, the choice, while not ideal, was clear. I would avoid the worst choice and what was sure to be a chaotic living arrangement with my dad. I would also sacrifice a good, safe, and disciplined life which would surely lead to stability, college, and a future. Instead, I would stay with Aunt Rita in Jersey City where even though we would live in a cramped apartment, I could still fend for myself and be a part of my sister's life. Jersey City was my home. My hood. It was what I knew. I also knew I had the Conte family's support and guidance. Jersey City would have me for a little longer.

CHAPTER 18

LIFE GOES ON

Me at 16 at Bobby's wedding.

It was 1991, and life went on. The internet was made available for unrestricted commercial use, and the number of computers on the net reached one million. Nirvana released their first major hit album, *Nevermind,* starting the grunge era in the '90s and slowly changing the face of rock from big hair and makeup-wearing rockers. On

ADRIAN ALVARADO

Wall Street, the Dow Jones Industrial topped 3000 for the first time.

I was in the middle of my freshman year in high school, a few months removed from burying my mother. In school I walked around in a fog. I didn't join any clubs, play football, or try out for the baseball team like I'd originally intended. Before my mom's illness, I was trying to be a normal kid. Even though I was always working, I had made time for football in my eighth-grade year, as well as baseball. Baseball and football were my sports. I pitched and played outfield in Little League, and I was captain and quarterback for my city's recreational tackle football team, "The Downtown Bulldogs. My goal was to try out and start for the high school freshman team, as well as pitch for the baseball team, but I missed football camp, and once I learned the cancer was terminal, I just didn't think about sports anymore—or anything else for that matter. Tony had convinced me that I had to take care of my pocket now. I was on my own, and I had to work and save up. "Nobody's gonna put a dollar in your pocket but you, Chino," Tony would keep saying on and on.

So, working at the pizza shop after school became my priority. When I had turned 14, Tony started to train me at the pizza counter serving slices, answering the phone, and working the register, which meant more hours and more money in my pocket. I began to settle into my new life. I was living with my Aunt Rita and waking up to my cousin's size twelve feet in my face every day. I crashed on the couch most nights. In the mornings, I always got up first to hit the shower before Marcus could get in. He had a long routine of turning the hot water on and letting the bathroom steam up while he sat on the toilet. My routine was a lot quicker; shower in two minutes and spend the rest of the time blow-drying my hair to perfection. Then, I'd slap on a little grease to hold it in place. I did my best to assimilate and go back to school after all that had happened the past year. I had missed about a month of school during the process. I was behind in class and behind socially from day one. A lot of my teachers understood my situation and gave me some slack, but the start of my freshman year was a blur. By spring, I was back to my normal routine of school and working at Tony's. But the situation around the block at Tony's pizzeria was getting worse. The tension with Tony and the pizzeria next door had intensified. The rumors about Tony and me didn't stop, and stress was escalating.

ADRIAN ALVARADO

CHAPTER 19

A PIZZA WAR

3 Boys from Italy and neighboring Tony's Pizzerias.
Photo by: Anthony Olszewski

Danny and Samo were mixed Italian and Polish local kids that Tony had grown up with. They were all around the same age, in their mid-twenties. Danny Stankowitz was a white kid shaped by his changing urban environment. He stood about 5'8" with a slightly portly build, short straight black hair combed back, a cratered face, and he talked with street slang. He lived around the corner on 3rd Street with his Puerto Rican girlfriend and baby momma. Danny had a brash demeanor and was the obvious ringleader on the block, selling coke from the bar across the street. He thought he was hot stuff. Samo was more low-key—the muscle. They always had a little entourage with them. I knew a few in their crew, kids my age, who were selling weed and coming out of the bar with their supplies.

Initially, Tony's Pizzeria started off without a hitch. Tony, Danny, and Samo had a mutual respect and minded each other's business. Tony wasn't an idiot. He grew up with these guys and knew all the characters. He understood how the block worked. He turned a blind eye to whatever didn't interfere with his business. The bar across the street, The Hudson Inn, was a dive bar with seedy clientele. The owner, Joe, an Italian guy in his sixties, owned that whole side of the block. He allowed local small-time dealers like Danny to use his bar as a cover for drug dealing. It wasn't uncommon to hear or see someone had overdosed at The Hudson Inn. I saw a man get pulled out once. It seemed he had overdosed on heroin. Guys were trying to keep him standing, yelling, "Make him walk!"

Joe was an old-school gangster type of guy. He did well for himself though. He lived right across the street from Tony's pizza shop with his family in one of the apartment buildings that he owned. He walked around his side of the sidewalk with a cigar in his mouth and a smirk on his face. He was quiet. I don't recall ever hearing his voice.

Tony shared some of their family history with me. The story goes that Tony's dad, Tony Sr., and Joe were friends back in the day, but something happened. Maybe gambling. Maybe women. I don't know. Tony would never go into detail. Even after Tony's dad passed, Tony always kept his distance from Joe and his two sons. Tony tried to play along and not be so uptight with them and the local boys on the block to avoid conflict. We all started off real cool. Nobody had beef with anybody. As the Italians say, everybody ate. Sometimes Samo and Danny would even help at Tony's and run food deliveries. It was all good. But Tony wasn't a huge fan of the movement on the block—still, as a local businessman, he had to tolerate it to some degree. It was a necessary evil. These guys lived around this block, and they could make Tony's life hard if he rocked the boat, but every man has his breaking point.

Danny started to take advantage of Tony's pizza delivery gig and started making drug deliveries of his own while dropping off pizza pies and meatball sandwiches. Tony got wind of this when one day, Danny told Tony he believed he accidentally threw away his stash of drugs in our garbage can. Danny was also taking an extra ten to fifteen minutes longer on his deliveries. I was there and remember it like it was yesterday. He asked Tony to let him dig through the garbage. Danny was in our back alley digging in the trash like a madman. Somehow, he'd thrown away his whole stash by accident or he was hiding it. Either way, he found it and came back from digging through the trash with a huge smile on his face, clearly relieved. "Whew, that shit was close!" he said.

Tony hated drugs. He despised them with passion. His own brother Paulie struggled with addiction, and Tony had seen the effect it had on his mother and his family. Tony always proudly boasted that he never smoked a cigarette or tried any drugs. He did not approve of this situation. It was one thing for it to be happening on the block, but it was eating him up inside that it was now in his store. We had begun to get more of his crew just coming in and out of the pizzeria. Avoiding the eyes of the police whenever they patrolled the block. Tony decided it was time to put his foot down and told Danny this was a place of business, and he didn't want drugs in his place. Danny didn't take that too well and they parted ways. Soon after, the rumors about Tony and me being gay began.

Danny and Samo joined forces with Patsy and 3 Boys Pizzeria next door and declared all-out war against Tony's Famous Pizzeria. They were always around the block and started delivering pizza for 3 Boys Pizza next door, and Patsy loved it. They also began to sway customers away from Tony's, saying the dirtiest things they could say about the place:

"It's dirty, don't go in there." "Their pizza sucks." "They are infested with roaches in there." "The owner is gay, and he likes teenage boys." All lies.

They started heckling and blowing kisses at us every time we walked past them. They never did it to our faces though, only after we passed them. Some of the so-called friends I grew up with started joining the fray. Danny and his crew would be outside 3 Boys Pizza every day after school. I had no choice but to walk by them every day and every day I would get heckled. "Psst, Chinoooo." Followed by the sound of a kiss. I started to dread this part of my day.

We knew things were getting serious when a chair was thrown down from the roof of our building, landing at the pizza shop's front door. Tony even started wearing a bulletproof vest and carrying his .38 special everywhere he went. It started to make me uncomfortable. If Tony was going through those measures to protect himself, that meant that I too was in danger. I was getting harassed as well, but I didn't have a vest to keep me safe from a bullet.

Tony's cousins from uptown started to hang with us during closing time and would escort us to the car after work. The tension was building on the block, and you could feel it. It was starting to affect business as well. Danny and Samo's tactics were working. Tony's business started to dip.

I did what Tony, and his family said to do and walked with my head high and did my best to not let any of this get to me. I knew who I was. But it was hard. Real hard. The rumors were starting to reach me at school. It was difficult enough to deal with it all at work, but now I had to deal with it at school. This was the only place I could be a teenager. The only place I didn't have to worry about threats, rumors, work, or drama. I mean, I was looking for love or lust and no girl was going to talk to me if she thought I was gay.

A significant part of me yearned for change. Once again, I began to feel trapped by the environment around me. The escalating drama at Tony's was stressing everyone out. Internally, I was still grappling with my mom's loss and detested being surrounded by constant turmoil. Despite my love for Tony and his family, I wanted to leave Tony's and everything else behind me, just to be alone, be a student. I didn't want to have to worry about work, saving money, rumors about my sexuality, drama, and responsibilities. I just wanted to go to work and go to school. Mind my own business.

I had to come to terms with the fact that I couldn't just leave the situation. I was already a part of this. Lines were already crossed. Even if I left, it wouldn't go away. I also needed the job. I needed Tony's Pizza shop, no matter what. On top of this, at home, I felt like a stranger living with my Aunt Rita. I wanted to move out already, but I couldn't. So, I had to keep working, keep pushing through. I couldn't depend on anyone to help me financially. Even though I was staying with my aunt, I paid for myself. She didn't have to worry about feeding me and putting clothes on my back. I already felt like a burden to her, and I refused to give her another reason to consider me one. Aunt Rita had already suggested I might have to move in with my father shortly after I moved in. The conversation about me having to leave quickly shifted when she started receiving a monthly check from my mother's social security. I never voluntarily saw a penny of that money the whole time I lived with her. She also started claiming me as a dependent, and because of it, we were able to get an apartment downtown closer to school and near the PATH train station to NYC. The living accommodation was better for all of us. Marcus and I still had to share a room, but at least now we had bunk beds. This move improved our living arrangements, especially compared to where we had been a year before.

 Despite our improved living arrangements, I still wasn't Rita's son, and her discontent with me was subtle but palpable. I remember the entrance to the apartment was near her bedroom, which didn't have a door. When I'd come home from work at night, I would first turn on the lights in the kitchen, go to the bathroom, wash my face, and get ready for bed. I had to pass by her bedroom to get to mine. Every time I walked by, she hissed or moaned about me turning on the light, flushing the toilet, or whatever little noise I made which inadvertently caused her to wake up. After a while, to avoid being a nuisance to her, I stopped turning the bathroom light on and taught myself to quietly pee on the side of the bowl to make less noise. I felt like I had to walk on eggshells every time I came into the apartment. In contrast, when Marcus got a night job at a warehouse, he would come in at midnight, turn on all the lights, and make himself a sandwich. She wouldn't say a thing. I got it. I accepted that she would never treat me like a son, and I also knew my living situation was temporary. I had already set a goal to move out as soon as I turned 18. If all I had to deal with was Aunt Rita's attitude to keep my promise to my mother and be around for my sister, then it was worth it.

I kept an eye on my little sister Shailin as promised. Shailin and Luis conveniently lived around the corner from the pizzeria on 2nd Street and Cole. He still had his city job and seemed happy and calm living with his daughter. He never remarried. Although I still held contempt towards him for his treatment of my mother, I still loved him and kept a good rapport with him. We had a mutual goal, and that was looking after Shailin. I made sure she always had something to eat, always had pizza or whatever she wanted. I'd buy her sneakers, the Nintendo Game Boy, give her money. Everyone in the pizzeria also kept an eye on her. Even though we didn't live together, we would see each other every day. We were still growing up together. Whenever Shailin came into the pizzeria, she would say, "I can't wait till I'm 18 so we can live together."

That was our goal, to live together again. We loved each other, and she knew her big brother was there for her whenever she needed me. I didn't know it, but as much as I was helping her, Shailin was also helping me. She was my why. She was the reason I was working so hard and the reason I didn't completely fall apart after mom's passing. She was helping me cope. I didn't have time to feel sorry for myself. Now that mom was gone, my focus was making sure the other woman in my life had everything she needed, that she felt loved and protected. She reminded me so much of Mom and having her in my life helped me get through.

As for the situation on the block, it was getting worse. There was a real looming danger, and at any moment, anything could happen. You could feel the tension between everyone on the block and us. We were all on edge at work. Tony was keeping it together, holding on to his faith that God would rectify the situation because, as he would say, "God's on our side, Chino." I, on the other hand, was ready to fight. Heckling had become a daily ritual for the thugs. I took solace in the fact that Tony was right about one thing: these guys were nobodies with nothing to lose. They were street punks and wannabe gangsters who were always on the corner and up to no good. "You're better than them, Chino. Keep your head high. You're working hard for yourself. Ignore them." Tony would keep repeating. Tony and his family had been a bedrock for me through my hardships. Despite his flaws, despite whatever anyone said about him, I loved Tony like a brother. I loved his family. I wasn't going to abandon them now when they needed me most. Tony Conte was the only constant person in my life that was interested in my success and offered me advice. I was a part of their family and ready to fight with them.

ADRIAN ALVARADO

The pizza war between 3 Boys and Tony's Pizzeria had taken a toll on both businesses. Patsy had been in the background encouraging Danny and his boys to create chaos for us by allowing them to come in and out of his pizza shop, running deliveries for him and no doubt their own side deliveries. Joe from The Hudson Inn wasn't helping either. He was subsequently benefiting from the drama and now had a partner in Patsy. It seemed like it was us against the block, 3 Boys, and 3 Boys was winning because now they also had The Hudson Inn, Samo, and Danny on their side. Maybe we were the bad guys, who knows.

Tony panicked a bit, changed his business approach, and started making huge 28" pizza pies, selling pizza slices for seventy cents that were double in size. On top of that, he started selling our regular 18" large pie for only five dollars if you picked it up. Patsy next door would match Tony's prices and even made his pizzas larger, but he couldn't make them as big as us. The neighborhood was always out for a good deal no matter who was beefing. Tony's started making a large profit during school lunches. High school kids jumped on the deal and packed the place.

The Jersey Journal and the Hudson County Reporter, our local newspapers, came out to do a piece about Tony's record-size pies and the pizza war. No one was making pizzas this big on an everyday basis. Nobody. Tony had a special pizza board made that was thirty-six inches wide. Whoever wasn't aware of the pizza war, now read about it in the paper. The publicity only heightened tensions. Seeing the story in black and white gave it legitimacy and a voice. Now the drama grew beyond a few blocks' radius. Things were escalating publicly, and all eyes were on us.

ADRIAN ALVARADO

CHAPTER 20

BOILING POINT

Me in Tony's kitchen at 15, holding a .38, Special.

It was the spring of 1991. The New York Giants football team were Super Bowl champions, the movie *The Silence of The Lambs* was released, Bryan Adams' "Everything I Do" held the pop charts for seven weeks, a group named Color Me Bad had a hit called "I Wanna Sex

ADRIAN ALVARADO

You Up," and on January 12th, Congress voted to authorize the Persian Gulf War. I had just turned fifteen.

The clock hit 3:05 P.M. and the school bell rang. I walked to my locker, grabbed my backpack, and headed to work as usual. I remember it being a beautiful warm spring day that quickly turned into a scene from Spike Lee's movie *Do the Right Thing*, except it wasn't a sizzling summer day in Brooklyn. We were in Downtown Jersey City, New Jersey, and, unfortunately, Rosie Perez wasn't my leading lady. I made a left off Jersey Ave onto Monmouth St, walking past the familiar nobodies that waited all day to heckle me. I ignore them as usual and saw Tony in the distance standing next to his car, a 1981 beige Lincoln Continental Mark VII with the boomerang on the trunk. Tony stood with his two brothers, Paulie, and Bobby. I nodded my head in acknowledgment and made my way to them. Seeing Tony and his brothers there gave me some comfort because they were looking out for me, but it also made me realize that anything could spark at any time, and I could be the fuse.

Tony's sister Marie was working at the pizza counter as usual. Marie worked lunches until I was ready to take over. I greeted her and headed straight to the bathroom, my sanctuary, and where I hung out while I got ready for my new shift. My duties at the pizzeria grew as I got older. I now worked at the counter serving pizza slices and answering the phone for deliveries, but I'd also still fold pizza boxes, run errands.

The bathroom at Tony's was like a country club locker room for me. I treated it as such. It was a tiny bathroom with a small sink and toilet, and it smelled like flour and yeast, but it was my quiet space. There was barely enough room to stretch my arms out, but this small bathroom provided me with privacy and a small break from reality. I made sure to use my bathroom time to relax and get lost in my thoughts. Unless someone really had to use it, or if a big food delivery order came in, everyone in the pizzeria knew to leave me alone when I was in there.

Before my shift, I would check myself out like any new teenager coming into his own. I'd take my time and make sure my hair was pristine before my shift. I would spend time pretending to be the Latin Luke Perry from the number hit show on TV, *Beverly Hills 90210*. I had shaped my sideburns just like Dylan. I'd put on my pizza-man uniform—white pants with a white button-down pizza collar shirt—and I made sure my hair was tight again. Then I'd practice random movie lines in the mirror. At fifteen, I had already decided I was going to make it in show business and become an actor one day. I was always working and rehearsing when I was alone with a monologue book I found in the library. I would have fun rehearsing in front of the mirror before my long, boring shift.

The first monologue I ever learned was one of Marlon Brando's most famous monologues from the movie *On the Waterfront*: "I could've been a contender." The movie was shot right here in Hudson County, in the small city of Hoboken. Come to think of it, maybe that's why I was drawn to it. Or it could have been that Tony's Pizzeria had the walls decorated with photos of the entire cast of the Godfather. Every day I had to stare at the headshots of Al Pacino and Marlon Brando's faces on the walls.

The line I practiced that day was much simpler than Marlon's agonizing monologue. It was a simple line from the movie *La Bamba*, starring the great Lou Diamond Phillips and Esai Morales. That was one of my favorite movies as a kid. Lou Diamond's character, the late great Rock & Roll legend Richie Valens, was performing on stage, and he suddenly stops playing his guitar, runs his fingers through his hair, and yells: "Ooh my hair!" And the ladies go wild!

After my imaginary standing ovations in the mirror, it was time to delve into my next fantasy. I would sit on the toilet and start flipping through the pages of my Hustler magazine. I knew it would be a matter of time before Tony interrupted, calling for me to cut the mozzarella cheese and start work. So, with my last few minutes, I delved deep into the heart and mind of Amber. Hello Amber! In that issue's centerfold, Amber was looking for real love and a guy who was tall, dark, and handsome. I had the dark features down, and I was 5'9" at the time, but growing, so maybe, I thought, I could have a shot with Amber. But before my imagination could take me too far, I was suddenly interrupted by a very loud and panic-filled scream. It wasn't the typical scream my Italian coworkers would fire off at one another to show their love when disagreeing with each other. This scream was different. It was a scream full of terror, and it ripped me out of Amber's tender love and popped me off the toilet like an ejection button. I quickly put the magazine down, pulled my pants up, and opened the door to find Marie yelling and trying to stop her oldest brother Paulie, who had just rushed in from the street. "Paulie, stop! What are you doing!" she screamed. I thought someone was trying to rob the place until I realized Marie was trying to stop him. Paulie was scrambling to retrieve Tony's shiny .38 snub nose pistol from the side of the refrigerator, where Tony kept it. *Why would Paulie be scrambling for Tony's gun?* I thought. I couldn't believe my eyes. Paulie was extremely intelligent, but he had his struggles with drugs. Paulie was never sober in public. He was always stoned on something so he would be the last person you would want to handle a gun in any circumstance.

Everything was moving in slow motion. Suddenly I found myself yelling at him as well, "Paulie what the fuck are you doing?!" Paulie grabbed the gun from the side of the freezer and the reality of what was going on hit me; *Tony must have snapped!* Marie tried her best to stop him but couldn't. Paulie stood at a solid 5'11" while Marie, although fit and feisty, was at best, 4'11". He easily slipped away from her petite frame. "Get out of my way! Tony needs help!" he yelled as he slithered past her.

ADRIAN ALVARADO

I stood at the door of the bathroom, frozen, still trying to grasp what was going on, yelling out, "Paulie put that back!" but there was no stopping Paulie. He ran past the pizza oven, made his way around the service counter, through the small dining area, three tables, a soda machine and two arcades. I called out in a last attempted plea, hoping I would reach him, and he would stop this insanity. "Paulie!" To my surprise, he stopped. I thought I had finally reached him. I could find out what was going on and talk some sense into him. Paulie quickly turned and looked me in the eyes. His face was one of acknowledgment and panic all at the same time. Denying my plea, just as quickly as he had stopped, Paulie turned and headed out the door with the .38 in hand. When he opened the door, sunlight flooded the restaurant as if he was entering a portal to a new dimension. Paulie hooked a right and disappeared to fulfill his mission.

Marie was in shock, frozen in place, and the sight of her staring into space made time seem to stop. I quickly snapped out of it and decided to chase after the gun. As I ran past Marie, I realized I didn't have my work sneakers on. I had jumped straight off the toilet when I heard Marie scream and hadn't put them on. The commotion outside was getting louder, and I had to make a quick decision: either put my sneakers on or chase after Paulie and the gun. This could be a matter of life or death. I decided my sneakers weren't all that important and followed him out the door.

As I walked through the portal of light and onto the street, everything continued to move in slow motion. This was it—it was finally going down. It felt as if this chapter in our lives had started like the base of a triangle and narrowed up to this breaking point. Tony and Samo were finally fighting, surrounded by a mob of people like an old classic fifties brawl. *Something must have set Tony off. This wasn't like him, I thought.* He was always the one telling me to take the high road. Tony always preached peace, prosperity, and God to me, like the good Catholic boy he aimed to be. But everyone has their limit—even Tony. Now, Tony was in the fight of his life, going up against a quiet, mean, and ready-to-kill Polish/Italian paisan.

The scene felt like being at an outdoor concert—everyone from the block seemed to be there, caught up in the frenzy. I saw Danny and his crew, along with customers from the bar across the street.

I moved through the crowd, blending in and scanning for Paulie. I could see Tony and Samo were squaring up like two gladiators. It was clear some blows had already been exchanged the crowd reacted with chorus of "oohs" and "aahs" as they sized each other up again. I was suddenly in the middle of the crowd, in shock. I couldn't believe this was happening! I mean, the tension and backstabbing had been brewing for years now. It had all the ingredients that were needed for a fight. I was ready to fight and be done with it all.

ADRIAN ALVARADO

While weaving through the crowd, I was keenly aware that any second one of Samo or Eddie's boys was going to spot me and want to get their licks in on me. I was ready, but we were also outnumbered three to one. My eyes were everywhere, as always. My main concern was looking for Paulie, but I also had an eye out for Tony just in case others jumped in. In my day, when two individuals decided to fight, you let them fight a fair fight, but these weren't the types of guys that I could trust to fight fairly.

As they were squaring off Samo suddenly unleashed a sidekick to Tony's stomach. Tony took it and didn't flinch, instead he taunted Samo. "Not hard enough!" he said. Tony charged with a left hook and connected. They tangled up and Samo got the upper hand and picked up Tony like Hulk Hogan lifted Andre the Giant in WrestleMania III, and body slammed Tony on the sidewalk. I saw Tony hold on and grapple, maintaining a hold on Samo and fighting like hell. Then suddenly, as expected, the crowd started getting hyped and someone snuck in a kick at Tony's head while he and Samo wrestled on the ground. Tony's brother Bobby stepped in and yelled at the young anxious misguided kid who kicked Tony to stop. "It's a fair fight," he yelled. Bobby wasn't much of a fighter. He knew it. Everyone knew it. Bobby, twenty-eight, a former racehorse jockey, was barely taller than Tony. Now Bobby was in the middle of a brawl, doing his best to referee and protect his brother. He yelled at the crowd, "C'mon, guys, fair fight!" At least there was one other person on Tony's side and looking out for him.

Everyone was focused on the fight, but I was in search of a gun. Although it was hard to believe the fight was happening, I couldn't get caught up. I made my way left around the circle of people when suddenly I heard a loud plop and thud. It was the distinct sound of knuckles smashing into a face and the head hitting the pavement. I had heard it before. It wasn't Tony though; he was still holding his own. It was ahead of me, and I hoped to God it wasn't Paulie. I followed the sound, slid through the crowd to find Paulie, on the street lying flat on his back with his mouth all busted up. He was out cold. One of Samo's brothers, Freddy, saw Paulie with the gun and sucker-punched him right in the face. Freddy was still over Paulie trying to grab the .38 from his hand. He seemed scared and confused about what to do now that he had the gun in his hand. Right then, I saw my opportunity and made my move. My instincts just kicked in and I dashed for the gun. A fight was a fight, no big deal, but if a gun was involved, the stakes changed. I reached out and ripped the gun from Freddy's hand. He was surprised by me but didn't put up a fight. He almost seemed relieved to give it to me. *Now what?* I must have had the same look as Freddy because I hadn't exactly planned this through. I was standing on the street, in the middle of a rumble with no sneakers on expecting to get punched, with a gun in my hands.

Just as the panic started setting in, I heard Bobby's voice calling me. "Chino!" he said as he grabbed at his keys motioning me to follow him. "Chino, Chino, this way Bro!" I followed him as he turned west on Monmouth Street towards Third Street. *Yes!* I knew where he was going. The family's apartment is around the corner from the pizzeria, on Third Street. Realizing Bobby's intentions, I followed him, keeping the gun low and running as fast as I could. Tony and Bobby used to take me to the shooting range, so I knew how to handle a firearm. Something told me to unload the gun as I ran. I figured if someone took it out of my hands, they wouldn't be able to use it. Bad idea. A bullet fell on the street. I stopped and turned back to pick it up only to find all eyes were on me. Someone yelled out, "Oh my God he's got a gun!" another person yelled, "Look at that little shit!" I couldn't blame them. They didn't know what my intentions were. They just saw the kid from the pizzeria holding a gun and grabbing bullets.

There was no time to explain myself and stopping to convince a blood-hungry crowd was not in my best interest. I turned and followed Bobby into the building down the block. Bobby quickly shuffled his keys, opened the door, and led me up the stairs to his mother's apartment on the second floor. He opened the door to the apartment, and I ran into the first bedroom and dropped the gun with bullets on the bed. "Good job, Chino!" Bobby said, with relief written all over his face. I was relieved too. I nodded but there was no time to chit chat.

FLIPPING MY SCRIPT

We had to check on Tony. If Paulie was knocked out cold, Bobby and I were here, who was looking out for Tony and what happened to Paulie? I quickly pivoted and headed back down the stairs to check on Tony. As I stepped back onto Third Street, I found myself alone and confronted by Eddie's boy Paquito who had followed Bobby and me around the corner. Paquito was headed straight for me, hyped up and ready for a fight. "Come on, Chino, you and me!" he yelled.

Paquito was a year or two older than me. His cousin Tito and I were best friends in grammar school. But now, Paquito was caught up in Eddie and Samo's riffraff and forgot himself. He was squaring up his arms to fight me. Without hesitation he rushed me. I instinctively dodged and tripped him making him fall to the ground; just like my uncle had taught me all those years ago. Finding himself unexpectedly on the floor only seemed to anger him. Paquito jumped to his feet ready to attack again only to find a face full of fist. This was my chance, and I threw punch after punch and connected just like I did the punching bag in the basement. He was going down. I was ready to unleash all my anger and anxiety on him. Until a fist smashed my head from behind and I staggered. I felt the heat of the blow going down my spine, but I got my bearings quickly, I had to. This was fight or flight. I saw two more guys coming at me. Paquito did not come alone. I was outnumbered and about to get jumped but I was not backing down. I knew this wasn't a fair fight, three against one, but I stood there ready to get some punches in and take a beating. I figured I'd might as well get it over with, but police sirens came rolling in and everybody scattered, including me. My fight would have to wait another day.

First, I ran with no place in mind but then I thought the safest place to go would be the police station where I'd have a fighting chance. At least there I would have backup, protection from the thugs. I made it to the JCPD East Police Station on Seventh Street and Erie in two minutes. It wasn't far from us.

When I arrived at the station, I stuck out because I was wearing my all-white work uniform. A few seconds later Danny walked in and started talking to the cops. He pointed towards me and said I had a gun. The cops looked up and brought me to a desk where they sat me down for questioning. They asked me questions about what happened. "Did someone have a gun?" I played dumb and stayed quiet. I was more concerned about Tony's well-being. They didn't push too hard. They couldn't. The gun was not on me, and I was a minor with no adult representation. They just let me go. It was Danny's word against mine. The cops had bigger fish to fry, and Danny wasn't exactly an upstanding citizen. As soon as he'd walked in one of the cops yelled his last name like he knew him, "Stankavich, what happened?" As I came down the stairs from being questioned, people from the neighborhood were being brought in for questioning including Tony and Samo. Soon after being brought in Tony fell to the floor in full-blown panic attack mode, pounding his fist and feet on the police station floor and foaming at the mouth. I watched him from the stairs above unsure if he was really having an attack or putting on a show. I saw some of the players from the fight coming in with smirks on their faces and soon after the Conte family. I slipped through the crowd, left and returned to the pizzeria. Nobody got arrested that day.

ADRIAN ALVARADO

CHAPTER 21

STILL BLOWING KISSES

Me at 15 leaning on our dough floor mixer and cheese shredder.

It was my Uncle Santos who taught me how to defend myself. He gave me a foundation during all those summers I spent in Puerto Rico. He taught me how to defend myself and showed me how to punch someone in the face whenever my personal space was threatened. We would spend the whole summer watching and talking about Bruce Lee movies, his techniques, and philosophy. "Be like water," Santos would repeat.

ADRIAN ALVARADO

Uncle Santos took me everywhere with him. We would play fight all the time. He would close his four fingers and make the shape of a spear, poking at my chest, arms, back, and legs. That shit would hurt, but I had to take it. He was toughening me up and showing me how to defend and withstand a little pain. After a while, I learned to block it and eventually stopped feeling the pain. He taught me never to look for a fight but always to be ready to defend and attack. Santos would say, "If a guy pushes you, you don't push back, you punch back! It's not a pushing contest. It's a fight." Fighting was not something I wanted to do, but knowing how to defend myself gave me the confidence I needed to survive.

After Tony and Samo's fight, nothing really changed. If anything, things got more awkward. Danny and his crew were still on the stoop in front of 3 Boys Pizza. All day. Every day. Doing the same thing—nothing. The pizza war between Tony and 3 Boys became a war of attrition. Both pizzerias competed by lowering prices to bring in the volume. Business sucked. More work, less money. The taunting and teasing were part of my everyday routine now. I didn't want to go to Tony's for lunch anymore, but he would always make me so I could help watch the soda machine. I started to hate it. It meant I had to pass by the punks on the stoop and get harassed, sometimes in front of classmates walking by. I was ready to fight Danny myself. I wasn't afraid of him. Danny Stankavich was Tony's age. A grown man. And here he was leading a pack of young men to harass a 15-year-old kid.

Danny's crew had a few new faces. He always had the dropouts and older kids with him. Now there were kids I grew up with hanging out with him. Former so-called "friends" of mine joining the fray. A kid called Omar was one of them. His skin was light brown with short, straight black hair, a long neck, sharp nose, and rat-like face. He stood next to Danny, smirking at me and looking as though he had found a new toy to mess with. Little did he know, I wasn't going to let him get away with it. If he thought he could act like the big boy and whistle at me, he had another thing coming. Omar was in my age range; I knew I could take him down. But my Uncle Santos' voice would pop in my head, and I would hear him say, "Don't be the attacker. You're outnumbered. Be smart. Catch him alone."

I wish Uncle Santos was here with me now, I thought. *This wouldn't be happening if he were here with me. He'd smack that stupid grin off Danny's ugly face,* I thought. But Uncle Santos wasn't here. He was on the island, three thousand miles away. I had confidence that I could hold my own against any kid or man my size who had anything to say about me to my face, but all I really wanted was to be left alone. I wanted to enjoy the high school experience and be involved in sports. I wanted to live in peace and get through the next few years so that I could move out on my own, take charge of my own destiny, flip my script, take care of my sister, and look out for my brother Richard.

The next day in the hallway at school, I heard someone call my name, then hiss and whistle as I left for lunch. "Psst, Chino." I knew who it was—Omar. I didn't turn around or acknowledge it, but it stung. It hit me harder than when Danny and his boys were doing it. Out in the streets was one thing but having him bring that shit to me in school and in front of my peers was not cool. *Shit!* I thought. To make things worse, a classmate, Gloria, had stopped me in the hallway earlier in the day to ask me if I was gay. I told her I wasn't and that anyone who was saying that about me didn't know me personally. I had no issues with anyone being gay, but it was making me angry that I was being bullied and harassed for being something I was not, and now I had to deal with it in school.

During lunch, I would let out my frustrations at the pizza shop. "Tony, I don't know how much of this shit I can take anymore! I'm gonna fuck them up!" I told him. Tony continued preaching the high road. "Keep walking with your head high. Those guys are not going anywhere in life, Chino. You are. Be smart. They're punks, we know that. Always in a group, alone, they're cowards. You know who you are," he spoke. "But they started doing it at school today, Tony. This kid Omar was in the hallway with a few kids starting to act the same way. This isn't good, Tony. I can't be dealing with this shit in class and in the hallways," I said. "I can't take it anymore, Tony. Something's gotta give."

Tony preached the same thing again, told me to calm down and not give in. I was over it. My hands were shaking with anger, and I wanted to fight for myself. I walked back to school alone like usual, fuming. My fists and my jaw were clenched the whole walk back to school. I felt my stomach twirling in a million directions and my heart was pounding out of my chest.

As I approached the west entrance on Columbus Street and the park, usually the busiest area during lunch before class starts again. I made my way to the door and guess who was standing there with a little crew waiting for me? Omar. He had a brazen look on his face, blocking my entrance as I tried to walk inside. I swear I saw red. Without thinking about it, I shoved him and swung, barely connecting. I didn't care if I got jumped. I had reached my limit. "Come on, let's go! Let's go!" I yelled with my fists up. Omar charged at me and swung. I ducked, turned, and put him in a headlock in one quick motion, spreading my legs apart for leverage. My uncle taught me well. He tried to jab my head and lift me up. I could feel I was stronger than him. He failed to lift me and started punching me in the back of my head, but I didn't feel any of his punches. Lucky for him, the school guards showed up and broke us up. "Whistle at me again, you punk! I'm gonna wait for you after school and kick your ass!" I shouted. The guards pulled me away and let me go. The guards weren't stupid. They knew who the bullies and troublemakers were in school, and I wasn't one of them.

Scuffles in my school were commonplace. A big chunk of Ferris High School's student body lived near or below the poverty line. There were a lot of rough and tough kids from broken homes like me. Later that afternoon, in between my seventh and eighth periods, I saw Omar in the hallways. I held back from charging him right then and there. That was a guaranteed suspension. Everyone knew better than to fight inside the school building. You had to be smart and wait to fight after school, but that didn't stop me from talking smack. "You hit like a bitch. You think you know me? I'll be waiting for you at three o'clock!" I barked. "Count on it!"

Omar woke up the Bruce Lee dragon in me. I wasn't holding back anymore. I felt energized and I was ready to fight him alone or with his crew. I knew there was a chance I might get jumped, but I didn't care. I had no choice; I knew what I had to do, and I was going to unleash all my pent-up anger onto Omar and all his chump friends that got in my way, no matter the risk. It was time to put up or shut up, and I couldn't wait.

High school could be an unforgiving place. Movies and TV shows reflect our society, and I'd seen enough movies like *Back to The Future* and *Revenge of the Nerds* to know that if you don't stand up to bullies, you're in for a long, tough ride and a life like George McFly. But George McFly was lucky. His son Marty had a friend with a time machine. I didn't. All I had at this moment was confidence, fighting skills, and knowledge. Boxing and fighting are all about weight class and height. You can't think you're going to always beat a guy bigger than you. You must be strategic when picking your opponent. Even though I wasn't afraid to fight Danny and his boys on the stoop, the reality was Danny was an adult. Fighting an adult like Danny or Samo wouldn't be a smart choice for a 15-year-old. But fighting anyone near my age who thought they could get away with trying to bully me in my school, well, that's another story. I already knew I was stronger than Omar. I felt his power in our short preview scuffle earlier. Senior or freshman, I didn't care; they had a fight waiting for them.

    Last period came along, and the school bell rang. My chest was pumping, and my hands were sweaty, but I was ready. I grabbed my books and headed to my locker. On my way there, I ran into my cousin Marcus in the hallway and told him what had gone down earlier. My cousin wasn't a troublemaker, but he and his boys had my back. I now had someone on my side in case his crew tried to jump me. I made my way to the back of the school's Christopher Columbus Street exit. Outside, a crowd was already gathering. Fight rumors spread fast in high school. I don't remember being nervous. Just angry. I didn't care what was going to happen. I looked down the block and saw Omar and about six guys hyping him up and instigating as they made their way toward me. Omar threw his hands up, signaling he was ready, but I wasn't going to attack first. I waited for him to approach me. I put my hands up, and once again time seemed to slow down.

As soon as he got within distance, I swung with a straight right to his nose and a left hook to his temple. *I got this. He's got nothing on me. Let's go!* Omar staggered back, surprised by the quick one-two, and in frustration, rushed me. I used the step aside, trip move, and next thing I knew, I had his head in my hands and pushed it down to meet my knee midair. I smashed my knee into his cheek, and he stumbled back. Blood started pouring from his nose. He was stunned. I stood there and gave him a moment to gather himself, but he hadn't had enough. He was getting his ass beat, and he knew it. Now he had something to prove, so he lunged at me again, this time pushing me to the school wall. I was tired, so we grappled at the wall for a minute. He slipped a right to my face. *Good shot.* Getting hit in the face gave me a jolt of energy and newfound anger. I tapped into my wrestling moves and performed a dip and spin. Omar was now in front of me. I picked him up, slammed him on the wall, and started punching him in the stomach hard. He went down, and once again I stepped back. That wasn't good enough for the crowd. Omar was down, bloody and beaten, but the crowd wanted more. He got up, acting like he still wanted to fight, blood streaming from his nose, but his eyes were saying something different. I stood in front of him at the ready, but he'd had enough. So had I. I'd made my point, and we both knew it. The crowd, on the other hand, was restless. I felt pushing, shoving, and grabbing. Everyone was fired up, but I wasn't fighting to appease the crowd. I was fighting to let Omar and anyone else that wanted to fuck with me know that they had another thing coming if they thought I was weak and someone to be played with. There was an unspoken exchange between Omar and me, and we left it there.

    The crowd kept pushing and shoving some more. My cousin and I were in the middle and thought we might get jumped when security came out and broke up the crowd. Good timing. Once again, I was saved by the authorities. Everybody scattered, and security pulled my cousin and me into the hallway. The same security guard from earlier asked me if I was ok. "You have blood all over your shirt," he said. "Yeah, I'm fine. It's the other guy's blood." I said. Omar had only connected with a good punch or two. I didn't have a scratch on me. My cousin Marcus and I waited inside until the crowd dispersed. Some of his friends showed up and walked me halfway to the pizzeria. I walked in, and Marie, Tony's sister, was there as usual and saw my bloodied shirt. "Chino, are you ok? Is that your blood?" "No. I got into it with that kid Omar. I couldn't hold it in anymore and kicked his ass."

    My victory didn't come without a little pain. I had a huge headache, and my hands hurt. I went to the back of the kitchen and made my way to the bathroom for a minute while my head pounded away. It was a good headache, though. A well-earned one. It felt good because from this point forward, if any of my peers in school or on the streets thought they could talk smack at me, they had another thing coming. One of the biggest mouths just got shut. I had to stand up for myself. Otherwise, the taunting would have never stopped. After my fight with Omar, he never whistled at me ever again. In fact, the next time I saw him, he showed me some respect by saying "what's up" to me. It's amazing what standing up for yourself will do.

When your challengers realize that you're not willing to lay back and take their shit, it makes them think. Nowadays, you can't settle a dispute with a fight, let alone a fair one. The fear of violent retaliation is real. There is no dignity in fighting anymore, and I don't encourage it. I appreciate Omar for taking the loss, moving on, and showing respect afterward. There's honor in that.

CHAPTER 22

BREAKING THROUGH

My first headshot at 17 yrs. Old. Junior year, 1993.

It was 1992. President George W. Bush was on the way out of office after one term. His infamous "Read my lips" quote didn't go too well. President Bush also underestimated a charming saxophone-playing southern playboy named Bill Clinton, who was on the way in. In Los Angeles, it was nothing but a "G-Thang,", with Dr. Dre and Snoop Dog. Police brutality was all over the news, and the Rodney King riots were in full effect. I was in the middle of my sophomore year of high school, determined to take control of my life.

    The tension on our block settled down a bit. Shortly after the big fight on the block Danny got arrested for selling coke, and his crew dispersed. Having two pizzerias next to each other was the norm now and we all had to coexist. I started to settle into a decent school and work balance. My home life was what it was at Aunt Rita's. I showed up to sleep, doing my best to be invisible. My Dad on the other hand, hit a rough patch. He seemed to keep going downhill after he was stabbed by his girlfriend Iris. He ended up getting locked up and spending a couple of years in prison. He never told me why. My dad was incarcerated throughout the end of my high school years and so was my brother Eddie. Eddie was on his own and in a worse situation than I was in since we lost our mom. He continued to hustle and struggle on the streets, as well as with his addiction. He'd be in and out of the Hudson County jail system for jumping the turnstile to the train, shoplifting, and petty crimes to support his addiction. Occasionally, he would stop by the pizzeria, and I'd feed him a slice of pizza and give him a few bucks. Eddie had burned every bridge in our family, and no one trusted him enough to take him in. All I could do was feed him when he was hungry. The pizzeria was still providing for my family as broken apart as it was. At the end of the day, we were both on our own. When I'd ask, he'd say he was staying with a friend. I didn't know much about how Eddie lived his life. He always did his own thing. He was a street survivor.

My grades were decent in school, I could always do better, but I did enough to get through. I was thinking about college, preparing to rent my own apartment, and move out of Aunt Rita's as soon as I turned 18. I still wasn't sure about what I wanted to study in college. I also started to drift away from Tony and his family as well. I just focused on doing my job, and that was it. Work was work. We'd had a good run, but the fight had changed us. Both Tony and my goals and visions of who we wanted to be were changing. Tony was stuck in his ways, afraid of life outside the neighborhood. He hated planes and never planned to get on one. He would say, "You could pay me a million dollars, and I won't get on a plane. Nah, you can keep 'em!" I would tease him and say things like, "What, you're never gonna go visit Italy? Your motherland? Travel the world? Come on Tony." He'd fire back, "Don't need to. If I can't drive or take a train, I don't need to go. God forbid something happens to that plane," as he made the sign of the cross.

I would just shake my head and tell him about all the places I was planning on visiting. "I want to travel the world. I'm going to be famous," I would say. Tony was stuck with the idea that we weren't meant to fly. "I'm not tempting God." *How was that tempting God, I would think.* I always thought it was hypocritical of him to say that. Tony would go on and on about how a heart and brain surgeon's hands were blessed by God. I would counter with, "You saying the pilot's hands aren't blessed? The engineers, the mechanics?" He would smile, shake his head and say, "You can keep them."

Tony and his family seemed content with living in their bubble, staying within their home's 12-block radius and never leaving unless necessary. God forbid Tony had to drive more than 20 minutes outside the city. I couldn't understand it. All I wanted was change. I began to wonder if a lot of the lessons Tony preached to me were based on fear. They were solid lessons: Work hard. Put money in your pocket. Don't trust anybody. But he never talked about enjoying life, falling in love, seeing the world. His main goal, his main purpose was to make money.

In the early years of Tony's pizzeria when things were going well, I would always be the one producing ideas on how to have fun. I would always beg Tony to close a little early and go out bowling. He would agree and Tony, Bobby, and our regular at the pizzeria Dominick and I would go. It's the only thing he would do besides going out to Diners all the time. Here I was, a 15-year-old Puerto Rican kid with these old school Italians, bowling in the Hudson lanes on RT 440 in Jersey City.

We had some good times at Tony's. On the weekends, sometimes when my mom was still alive and hanging at the social club, Tony, Bobby and Dominick would take us uptown to Greenville where his Uncle Joey, Vinny and four cousins lived. Vinny was the one who told me I wasn't a real American. He was a good kid and lived there with his two brothers and sister. We always had a good time. It's where I got to relax and be a kid sometimes after work. Vinny was 18, and his youngest brother Dom was a year older than me. They had a game room set up in the basement which included all the latest gaming consoles like Genesis and Super Nintendo. Dom, Vinny, and I would play Madden football, NHL hockey, and chess for hours. Vinny taught me how to play chess. Their mom Marie was straight from Italy. She would always come down at midnight and take out some leftover lasagna or baked ziti, and we would tear it up. She would always squeeze my cheek with a big smile and ask me, "You want amor lasagna Gino?" I went from toasting spaghetti on my stove when times were tough to eating the best homemade authentic Italian lasagna.

  We would all sit at the table and eat together. Tony sat where his dad used to sit, at the head of the table and across from his Uncle Joey. Tony's dad was the oldest before he passed. Uncle Joey, a retired sheriff, would come down and chat it up with us. Dominick, was over 70 years old, always hung out in the pizzeria with us and was always with us after hours at the diner whenever we went out to eat. He was a retired gravedigger who was divorced three times with no kids. He was about five-foot one with silver hair and sharp features. A retired Italian playboy who wore a different tailored suit every day with a matching hat, shoes, and the occasional gold-plated belt. Dominick was a character. Tony, Bobby, and his cousins loved to get a rise out of him.

Dominick was funny when he got excited. They also loved egging me on to get Dominick going.

Dominick and I had a rapport every time the subject of Italian American ingenuity came up at the Pizza shop. Tony and Bobby would start by stating all the great Italian painters, sculptors, and actors in American culture. Bobby with a mischievous smile would whisper to me on the side, egging me on. "Chino, tell Dominick how the Italians never did anything for this country." I'd play along and wait for my spot to say to Dominick, "What did the Italians ever do for this country Dom? You got a couple of famous paintings, a few sculptures and two actors: Pacino and De Niro, who else?" Dominick would turn red and start foaming at the mouth and yelling at me saying, "The Italians built this country! We went to war. We built the roads!" On and on. I would shoot back, "Did you build the roads yourself Dominick?" Then Tony, Bobby, his cousins, and the whole table would just burst out laughing as I hyped up Dominick and we went back and forth, working on my improv. It was our thing, and we all laughed.

I learned a lot from my extended Italian family. They were there for me, and I was there for them. If we were our own mafia, the events after the fight and the incident with the gun would have made me a "made man" with the Contes. Tony and his family would always tell me that I helped prevent a tragedy. Tony could have gotten in serious trouble if the gun was fired, and God forbid killed someone. Pulling it out alone would have been a felony. Tony and his family looked at me differently after that. I was one of their own now. Even Tony's cousin Vinny went out of his way to praise me in his own way. "You're all right Chino. You're not a typical Puerto Rican," he would say with a smirk. I shot back of course, "Thanks, Vinny. You're not a typical Italian either. You didn't surrender as soon as I showed up. Oh!", a veiled historical reference to say that Italy has surrendered in every world war. I never backed down or let them slide with any derogatory comment that came out of their mouth. I must say, the Italians always kept me sharp.

But things change. Life changes. I understood this about life now more than ever. Back in the pizzeria, business was up and down. I had made it clear to Tony that moving into my junior year, school and school activities would be my priority over the pizzeria. I mean, I still understood I had to work and make money. Nobody was going to hand me anything. I just didn't want the rest of my high school life to revolve around the pizzeria anymore. I was taking more control of my life and life choices.

One day I was on the bus returning from a school field trip. I was beginning to snap out of my funk and got more involved in school and paying more attention to my options. Sitting next to me on the bus was my future best friend for life, Israel. Izzy was a tall 5'11"-6' Puerto Rican kid with a sharp nose and dark curly hair. We had attended the same elementary school and graduated together in the 8th grade. We knew each other but had never connected until this day. It was the end of the school year, so we sat there on the bus reflecting about our year and our upcoming class options for our junior year. Izzy went on about how he was on the basketball team and the drama club. I snapped my head back and said, "Wait, what? We have a drama club in school?" Izzy was an actor as well, "I've been taking it since freshman year," he said. "I love acting!" I responded, "I used to do it all the time in grammar school." I told Izzy about the play I did when I was in the 3rd grade here in our high school. He told me to make sure and sign up for Mr. Wonder's class junior year. It didn't surprise me that I didn't know about the drama class or any other school activities. I was still recovering from my mental fog after my mother's passing and the pizzeria drama. I was always at work which didn't leave much time to be socially plugged in at school. After all the drama on the block, I needed a fresh start.

    I got home that night and immediately looked at all my available classes again with new eyes. I signed up for Drama 101 as well as a History of Film class. I even walked on the varsity football team, went to football camp, and made the team as a backup quarterback and back up third string defensive back. The football bug was short-lived once I got hit by my friend Rodelle Dupree, who later became a red shirt linebacker at Ohio State. I said to myself, nah, I'd rather act like a football player in a movie one day. My football bug lasted one season.

Drama class was where I would thrive. I met Mr. Wonder that year and he would change my life forever.

ADRIAN ALVARADO

CHAPTER 23

MR. WONDER

Theater Arts class of 1994. Mr. Wonder (downstage) directing the rehearsal for the Spring musical *Li'l Abner*.
James J. Ferris H.S. 1994 yearbook photo

Mr. Don Wonder had a personality that fit his name. He had a big Broadway smile, and his hair was a shiny dirty blonde turning white with a combover. He stood about 5'11" with a pear-shaped physique, and his high tenor voice projected and reverberated through the back of the room. "Ladies and gentlemen, welcome to drama class! I am Mr. Wonder."

The room was set up like a small theater with tiered chairs. There was a black grand piano in the middle of the room, and Mr. Wonder would start the class by playing some Broadway show tune intros. Then he would gather us all around the piano and teach us vocal warm-ups. Izzy was in the class too, and I immediately felt at home. I knew after we started that this is where I wanted to be for the rest of my life. Not a junior in high school but an actor, around other actors, playing, pretending, creating.

The first lesson in class was pantomiming. Pantomiming is like being a mime, acting and moving without words. Mr. Wonder made us all pretend we were breaking into an apartment through a window. Ha, based on my experience, I was confident I would nail the exercise. My boy Izzy was right; I was lucky to sign up for drama class. Being in the class reminded me of when my mom used to dress me up, and the local Halloween contests I won that one year. The room also brought me back to the 3rd-grade play. I couldn't believe I had been that withdrawn. Now there I was, in the same room! I felt like the universe had brought me back home, to the arts. The knowledge Mr. Wonder shared was invaluable. He was always generous and happy to share the way. He himself was a professional Broadway actor in his heyday and would share stories of auditioning in the city and the audition process. He always said he was finishing his tenure as a teacher and then going back to Broadway.

Mr. Wonder was a great piano player. He knew all the show tunes and could sing them all. He also directed all the musicals plays in school, and he clearly loved what he did. Towards the end of my junior year, I told Mr. Wonder that I wanted to be an actor. "This is what I want to do. I want to be an actor." "I'm sorry, Adrian," Mr. Wonder responded sheepishly and laughed.

I had a lot of questions. "Where do I start? What is an agent? What do I need to do?" Mr. Wonder answered all my questions. I depended on some of my teachers for help. Ms. Mahoney, my junior year English teacher, took notice that I was in drama and went out of her way to help me. She made me aware of my diction. I had a thick Jersey street accent, and she made me realize how broken my English was. She challenged me. I can recall her advocacy for my understanding of speech and dialect. She told me, "Adrian, you have a lot of potential. If you're going to be an actor, you must be aware of your diction and how you speak and sound so that you can diversify your talents." Ms. Mahoney was a tall brunette – and the prettiest teacher in school. She gave me homework and told me to rent and watch a movie called *My Fair Lady* starring Audrey Hepburn and Rex Harrison, and I did. After watching that movie, I became aware of my diction and pronunciation. I became more versatile. I became a student of drama and started reading Shakespeare regularly at home. I'm grateful to have had several teachers that were passionate about their job and went above and beyond to help me. Another one of my English teachers, Mr. Corcoran, was a surfer and an artist at heart. Everyone called him Mr. C. He taught me about the diligence of Shakespeare. He would always have me read one of the leads when it came time to read the plays aloud in class. All my English teachers did, whenever we read *Macbeth*, *Julius Caesar,* or *King Lear*. Mr. C. also encouraged me to write a book one day. This book.

That first year in drama class, I auditioned for the spring school musical, and I got my second high school role. I played Hugo in the musical *Bye Bye Birdie*. My boy Israel got the lead as Conrad Birdie. I had the best time rehearsing and expanding my social circle. I started to interact more with girls and had my fair share of crushes. I was also attracting some crushes of my own. I realized being an actor in a school play where you get to kiss the girl can really improve your social game. I changed my routine and stopped going to work immediately after school and stayed longer for rehearsals. I worked it out with Tony that I would just work the dinner rush and weekends all day. The following year I got the lead in the spring musical as *Li'l Abner*. That year I had several lady volunteers wanting to practice stage kissing. I happily obliged. What? You can never over-rehearse. It's true what they say about co-stars developing a crush for one another. My co-star Jenny and I ended up going to the prom together. Israel and I went half on a limo.

FLIPPING MY SCRIPT

Mr. Wonder really was a treasure for me. He genuinely answered all my questions and prepared me for a lifelong adventure in acting. He showed me how to prepare my resume and what to expect at auditions. Little nuances that I still use to this day like not waiting in rooms with other actors. Mr. Wonder showed me a way out, and I ran with it. The first step to getting out there, he said, would be to pick up two acting editorials that were a staple in the industry. One was called *The Ross Report*, a monthly publication listing all the talent agents in New York, Chicago, and Los Angeles. It listed their name, address, what they were looking for, and if they were accepting new talent.

The other was *Backstage*. *Backstage* was the go-to editorial for all acting and performing information. Still is. *Backstage* had everything I needed to get started; inside, I could find photographers to take my headshots as well as other acting classes and info. It had all the casting breakdowns from Broadway, TV, dance, and film. You could submit yourself. *Backstage* came out every Thursday.

I was fortunate to have New York City nearby, as it is a haven for the arts and whatever you aspire to become in life. Lucky for me, I lived in Downtown Jersey City, which was only two stops from the mecca of arts and acting, Manhattan. There was also a newsstand by the Grove Street train station in Jersey City that carried the magazine. I quickly found a photographer in NYC and took my first black-and-white headshots at 17.

ADRIAN ALVARADO

I paid around $200 plus $40 for the makeup artist. I picked out my wardrobe and took myself to the city for the shoot.

Every Thursday was dedicated to getting myself up extra early and grabbing a *Backstage* magazine before they ran out. As soon as I had it in hand, I'd start going through all the theater, TV, and film breakdowns in New York. I looked for all the descriptions that fit a 17-year-old Puerto Rican, Hispanic kid. I would highlight each one, write the address on manila envelopes, and add my headshot and resume. I fluffed up my resume with all my theater readings of Shakespeare in my English classes and the plays I'd acted in. I would then mail them all out. I'd send out anywhere between 5 and 10 envelopes a week. It was a good thing I had a job at the pizza shop. Copies of headshots, stamps, and envelope expenses added up!

CHAPTER 24

A LETTER FROM COCA

Coca cooking at the Patillas River in Puerto Rico while I serenaded her with my guitar.

The island was left unattended. The pearl of the sea. Her gold was taken. Her sugar's monetary value was depleted. Her beaches, privatized. It's people, poked, tested, and sent to war. This Pearl of the Sea, this key to the new world, left alone in the dark.

ADRIAN ALVARADO

My last two years of high school were much more enjoyable than my first two. I established great friendships, and I started to come into my own. As soon as I turned seventeen, I got my driver's license and that enabled me to make more money by making food deliveries at Tony's. I was also now old enough to be a pizza man now and was making the pies regularly. So, I would make the pies and deliver them. I could do it all.

I saved as much money as I could and was preparing for graduation and renting my own place. I planned to study drama and communications in college. I applied to local colleges and got accepted by all. I chose New Jersey City University in 1994. I turned eighteen in April, right before my high school graduation, and instead of moving into a dorm, I moved into my own apartment. I was serious when I said I wanted to leave Aunt Rita's. I didn't even tell her until she came home one day, and I had removed all my belongings from my room. She was a bit shocked that I pulled it off.

As it turned out, an apartment had become available in Tony's mom's building, and they were kind enough to rent it out to me for $350 a month. It was a one-bedroom apartment above Tony's mom's apartment and below Bobby's. My next-door neighbors were a Polish family, a couple, and their teenage son. I had never been so happy in my life. I had finally done it. I was living on my own. The freedom to come in and out whenever I wanted, to be comfortable, be messy, to cook for myself and not have to feel like a stranger. To pee standing up!

My Aunt Maritza drove all the way from Dayton, Ohio, to attend my graduation. She had a surprise with her—my Grandma Coca. I remember breaking down when I first saw her. I didn't realize how much I'd missed her. A lot of time had passed, and a lot of things had happened since we'd last seen each other. I was different now. Her little Chuchin had grown up and been through some things. I was fully Americanized, having just survived my American battles on the streets and at home. Somehow, I had left all my memories of my childhood in Puerto Rico and my grandma behind the last few years. My life and everyday struggles in Jersey City streets did their best to strip me of my identity and heritage—of my Puerto Rico.

I remember apologizing to her for not calling and for being distant. It wasn't my intention at all. I was just caught up and taking life day by day. As soon as I sat next to her and hugged her, I went back in time to my childhood. The smell of her skin. Her girly smile. I felt a renewed connection, and I promised her that I would call her more often and visit her again. Seeing her again breathed new life into me. It made me realize that I wasn't as alone as I thought. She was always a phone call away.

I started my college orientations a week later. I selected all my college courses and immersed myself in acting, taking movement and speech classes. I got to focus solely on being a student for the first time in my life. I still had to work more than the average student body to support myself, but I was already used to that. I met some of my lifelong friends my freshman year like J.R. and Big Adrian and met my college sweetheart, Cindy. We met during orientation, and I immediately fell in love with her. Cindy had long wavy brown hair and curves for days. She was the most beautiful girl I had ever met. It took me all summer to get a date and a kiss from her. It helped that I had my own apartment, a dollar in my pocket, and a car available. Tony would let me borrow his Lincoln whenever I needed it for school. By the end of that summer, I convinced Tony to co-sign a new car for me. I financed my first car at eighteen, a 1992 cherry red Volkswagen Jetta.

  I was still actively submitting myself for auditions through *Backstage* while I was in school and looking for representation. Through my submissions, I found a manager, Art Massei. Soon I booked my first modeling job. It was an ad for the US Post Office. Guess what I played in the ad? That's right, a pizza delivery man. They had me dressed almost exactly like I dressed at Tony's. Stripe white and red shirt with white pants. The ad was of me delivering some pizza pies in a stairwell; its tagline was "Isn't it time to take a step in the right direction?"

  I kept up with my weekly submissions and booked my first two short educational films in the city and my first network television extra role in an ABC show called *City Kids*. Once the semester began, I immersed myself in the theater program and participated in my first college productions. A classical Molière play called *Learned Ladies* where I secured the role of Clitandre. My first foray into classical theater. I would also book my first supporting lead in a movie. It was a vampire horror film called *Sleepless Nights*, directed by William Hopkins and produced by Howard Nash who cast me. I played the lead vampire's mortal familiar.

Eventually, I left Tony's Pizzeria and started working at a place in Nutley, as a pizza man. I worked at a few various places. Tony and I had been through a lot together, and I needed my space. He made it clear I always had a job with him no matter what. We were always going to be family. He taught me a lot of skills, and I used them all, even still.

At eighteen, I flipped my script. My life wasn't perfect, but I was okay with that. It was my life. My own. My goals as a kid never really changed. Life dealt me some curveballs, but the goal was still the same. To succeed and change the cycle of poverty and dysfunction and make it in acting. I was already making it in acting in my mind. I was auditioning and doing what I loved.

My dad Felix and brother Eddie were still battling their own demons. My brother kept fighting to stay sober and maintain a steady job but would eventually go to prison for a few years. Around this time my dad got out of prison. When he got out, he had nowhere to stay and moved in with me. He was on parole. That time we spent together was when we started to get to know each other for the first time and our father and son relationship truly began. I was out in school and working most of the time, but we would take time to eat together. He would cook and I would start engaging him about who he was and our past. I took him in for about six months until he found a place of his own again. His plan was to move back to our house in Puerto Rico for good with his new girlfriend Lola.

I was still watching my sister Shailin and making sure she always had what she needed. I always did my best to keep her safe. I also began taking a bigger role in my brother Richard's care and took control of his guardianship shortly after my eighteenth birthday.

That fall, my Grandmother Coca sent me a letter. I still hold on to today. In it, she reminded me of who I was and how much I was loved. That I always had a home in Puerto Rico. That the island still belonged to me. Grandma started the letter by telling me to never forget about Puerto Rico and her love for me. She wrote that I wasn't alone even though I might feel that way. That she understood why I became distant after my mother's passing, but now it was time to reconnect to my roots. To come back home. That I was Puerto Rican. Her grandson. Her Chuchin.

Reading that letter broke me down. Still does. It revealed to me how lost I was and reminded me of my identity. Who I was and my roots. I was Puerto Rican. Something I had been seeking and trying to define for some time. I couldn't quite understand what was missing, but there it was. Written in my grandma's Spanish, almost illegible, handwriting. She wanted me to remember that I came from love, from her, from my mother's love, sacrifice, and legacy. That was all that I needed to know to understand myself, to love myself and where I came from. The good, the bad, and the ugly.

    A few months later I kept my promise and took a trip to visit Grandma Coca in Salinas. I booked a ticket through a travel agent and was able to rent a car with the help of my stepmom Zuly. I landed in San Juan and with a map in hand found my way down through the mountains to grandma's house in El Barrio Coco. There was no GPS back then. Finding your way involved pulling over to study a map or asking a local, "Which color house do I turn at?" It was dusk as I arrived. I parked the car in front of grandma's house and just sat there for a moment. All the memories of my childhood came pouring back. I remembered that happy little kid with dirty knees climbing the mango trees and catching small trout in the canal. I felt peace. I felt at home. And I also felt my mom.

    I couldn't help but smile as soon as I saw the tall, lanky silhouette of my Uncle Santos. He looked the same. He was a little older now but had the same smile and gangly walk. I hugged him and asked for his blessing. "Bendición," I said. "May God bless you and may the Virgin Mary accompany you," he replied in Spanish. We hugged it out and it automatically felt like old times. Soon I heard that familiar rambunctious laugh. There she was, Grandma Coca. We were back together again in Puerto Rico. Grandma immediately went to the kitchen to serve me a plate of rice and beans and roasted chicken. Homegrown chicken of course. Then we sat on the porch all night listening to the crickets and coquis, talking and catching up on my shenanigans. There was no explaining to do. It wasn't needed. Grandma was just happy to have her Chuchin back home. I remember thinking to myself, I'm never letting go of Puerto Rico again, this feeling of home. It will always be here when I visit. No matter what.

The next morning, like clockwork, the roosters made their call. It felt like I never left. I immediately got up and went to the back porch to feed the chickens like I did when I was a kid. The plan that morning was for Uncle Santos to drive me up the big mountain to Aibonito to visit my mother's grave. We left after breakfast. Grandma passed on making the trip, so it was just my uncle and me. But before we made our way up the mountain, I walked through the old neighborhood to visit our old house. Mom's old dream home. I made my way down Calle Celso Barbosa, passing by my old school, walking along the old now dried-up river canals I used to conquer when I was a kid, passing by the church I was baptized in and making a left to our old house on Calle Serafin Pabon. There it was. It looked the same. I was out of the loop for a while, but I learned it had been rented again. My Godfather Roberto was handling all of it and made sure the house was paid off. He saved it from getting abandoned.

My grandmother would then advise me to never let that house go. That it belongs to you and your sister. That the house will always be here for you. I assured her I would and have kept that promise.

My Uncle Santos and I made the trek up the mountain to Aibonito and found our way to the cemetery called El Campito by asking locals. It was tucked in the hillside. Once there, I remembered exactly where we buried my mother. When we buried her, I made sure to take a mental picture of a landmark I could easily recognize upon my return one day. Her plot had a beautiful native hibiscus flower tree near it. I looked for that tree and sure enough, the tree was still there and blooming. I walked towards it and found my mother's plot.

My uncle walked back to the entrance to give me some time alone with her. It was a perfect sunny day. The tropical air was warm and sweet. I placed the flowers I'd brought her down and just sat there with her for a bit, talking to her. It had been a minute since we were this close. I brought a guitar with me. I purchased it when I first moved into my apartment. I picked up playing the guitar as a hobby to keep me company. My intention was to serenade my mom, and I did just that. I played a little for mom and talked to her. I told her that Shailin and Richard were doing well and how Eddie was still Eddie. I told her I missed her and that I was studying acting and pursuing my career like I'd promised. I didn't realize how much I'd missed her and wished she was closer so that I could connect with her like this more often. But I knew what she would have said in return. She would have reassured me that she was with me everywhere I went.

It was time to say my goodbyes again, but this time I felt different. It wasn't the end. I had a newfound vigor for life. I was a man now. I knew I could come back and visit her and grandma whenever I wanted. I could come touch her. Her spirit would always be with me and here on the island's beaches whenever I landed. Knowing that, feeling that, gave me comfort.

Since we were in my mother's hometown, I was able to see my Grandparents Estelle and Alberto, they were older, frailer, and just stayed in the house mostly. I thanked them and asked for forgiveness for not being around. My Grandma Estelle was her usual self and quiet and just gave me a small smile. She looked like she had a deep sadness in her after her loss. Alberto just smiled like usual and took me out for a shot of rum.

I was also able to link up with my mom's sister Dahlia and one of my cousins, Veronica and Glory. We went out for a bite, and she drove us along the mountain countryside of Aibonito as we reminisced. I will never forget the connection I felt when I saw those beautiful mountains where my mother was born. It was perfect. That night, we danced salsa and merengue and reconnected to my roots in Aibonito. At one point, we were dancing, and I had to excuse myself and run to the bathroom. I was suddenly overwhelmed with emotion. My spirit was full. This was the first time in my life that

I'd cried, and it felt good. I was happy. Being here in Puerto Rico, visiting my grandma and dancing with my aunt, uncle, and cousins gave me a joy that I'll never forget. The emotions I felt were confirmation of what I needed to do. I needed Puerto Rico, and Puerto Rico needed me. It would always be a part of me. I wanted this feeling to last forever.

The next morning, the plan was to go to my grandmother's favorite river in Patillas. We got up early, and after breakfast, we headed to the river for the day. Grandma came prepared to make a turkey stew over a fire. The fire pit was next to the river under a canopy. My uncle and I brought hammocks and put them up between two trees. The river was beautiful—narrow and surrounded by lush tropical plants. You could hear all kinds of birds chirping in the background. My guitar came with us. At the time, I could only play a couple of chords well, but I showed them off to my grandma and she loved it. We would spend our entire day eating grandma's delicious stew next to her favorite river and sharing our love for each other while I played my guitar badly. It was great.

I spent the following day with my dad and grandmother. My dad was settling into his new life after his probation ended. Grandma requested that we visit Old San Juan together. We drove up and walked through the old cobblestone streets. They gave me a tour and shared all they could remember of the time they lived there. We walked down Calle Luna and passed by grandma's old apartment. I stopped at the corner where my dad shone shoes as a kid. It was magical. I learned after spending time with my family in Aibonito, walking the 500-year-old cobblestone streets of Old San Juan with my father and grandmother, and that day by the river in Puerto Rico with my grandmother and my uncle defined what it meant to be Puerto Rican for me.

Being Puerto Rican just means that you love your family, embrace your culture, accept both the good and bad of your history, and never forget where you come from. It means advancing your family and your community and striving to be the best person you can be. Nothing more, nothing less. We're Puerto Rican regardless of where we're born. Our DNA says so.

This was the best trip of my life. It brought me back to what I had forgotten and where my love of life first began. When it came time to head back to Jersey, I took my time saying goodbye to Grandma Coca. I headed back home with renewed confidence and a real sense of myself. My identity and spirit were free to begin my college journey and pursue my Hollywood dreams. Life was still a grind, and my journey was just beginning but, in my mind and soul, I knew that if I had life and purpose, I was going to be fine.

My pursuit of acting would eventually take me to Hollywood, California, with nothing more than a suitcase and $2,000 in my pocket. In my mind, failure wasn't an option. I still had promises to keep to my mom and myself, and no matter what cards or narrative the world wanted to give me, I was going to play them and flip them to my advantage. At the end of the day, I am the son of a hustler, and like my dad, Jersey City Felix, you must play with the hands you are dealt and keep playing the game. If your cards are marked, just grab new ones. It's all part of flipping your script and drafting your own story.

THE BEGINNING

ADRIAN ALVARADO

FLIPPING MY SCRIPT

ACKNOWLEDGEMENTS

To my beautiful wife, Diana Perez-Alvarado: You've had my back since the day we met. Your love, belief in me, and unwavering support are the reasons for any of my accomplishments. This book wouldn't exist without your encouragement, commitment, hard work, and love and creative spirit. Thank you for choosing me. I love you, baby.

To my beloved children, Sebastian and Natalia: Your laughter, curiosity, and love inspire me every day. This is for you, with all my heart. May you always chase your dreams and know that you are my greatest joy.

To my late mother, Nilda, brother, Eduardo and Richard: You have shaped my life in profound ways, compelling me to share your stories. You are my guardian angels, and I hope I'm making you proud up there in the stars. Rest in peace. I love you.

To my dad, Felix Alvarado Santiago: Dad, in the end, you were there for me and your grandchildren. Thank you, and I love you.

To the father who raised me, Luis Diaz: Thank you for stepping up and accepting me as your son. I forgive you. Rest in peace.

To my vivacious sister, Shailin: My salsa partner, my little sis, and my humble beginnings of hope. I love you. This book is your story as well. I hope it sparks a window of reminder of the love Mom had for you.

ADRIAN ALVARADO

To my grandmother, Atilana "Coca" Santiago: Your impact on my life lives on in my children.

To Titi Migdalia Ortiz—Bendición: Thank you, Titi, for always welcoming me and my family back home to my mother's home in Aibonito. Rest in peace.

To my Aunt Hilda, thank you.

To my Aunt Carmen, thank you for the family history you provided.

To my Aibonito family Monica, Veronica, Gloribel, Noelle, and Gabrielle. Thank you for always welcoming me back to Puerto Rico. Love you.

To my cousins Patricia and Micheal. Thank you.

To my beautiful sisters: Wajima, you kept me focused in the early years and believed in me. Thank you. Zulisha, you have been a steady, confident artistic guiding force. Zulisa, my homie, my confidant, and my muse—I'm grateful for you always having an ear and an open mind to our conversations. Janisha, we've connected through our love for the arts. I'm glad we found each other.

A big shout-out to my hometown of Jersey City: My city showed me everything—the good, the bad, and the ugly. Ultimately, I chose to see the good, and there was plenty of it.

To my Italian family: Thank you for taking me in and treating me like one of your own.

I am deeply grateful for my Aunt Maritza Santiago: My rock. The Santiago rock! The pillar of the familia. Your leadership and strength have always been paramount in our journey. Thank you for always taking care of your familia and your Chuchin.

To my Uncle Santos Reyes: te quiero. Thank you for taking care of Grandma Coca and for always being there for me, taking me under your wing during those summers in Puerto Rico. You taught me how to defend myself and gave me the confidence I needed as a man.

To my (Titis) Adelaida Reyes and Monse Reyes: You always greeted me with a smile and kisses. Love you! Bendición!

I am thankful for my second mother in life, Zuleika Alvarado: Thank you for always treating me like your son. Your strength, courage, and accomplishments are an inspiration to our family.

A big thank you to my in-laws, Raphael Perez and Antonia Fuentes: Thank you for bringing such a beautiful person (my wife) into this world. I'm so happy you did.

A shout-out to my brother and sister-in-law, Raphael Perez and Sarah Perez: Thanks for always supporting us and being there when we needed it most.

To my boy and best friend in life, my brother from another mother, Israel Acevedo: My dude, thanks for always being there for me. The best part of my childhood was the times we spent time together.

To my brother, Johnny Derisi: Thanks for always encouraging me, believing in my acting and comedy goals, and telling me I belong.

ADRIAN ALVARADO

To my brother, Adrian "Big A" Rodriguez: Thanks for driving me everywhere and hitting me up with cash when I was struggling as a young actor.

To my brother, J.R. Schaler: Thanks for making me go to that party in the city where I met my gorgeous future wife, D, and for always being a faithful friend.

My boy Hannibal Luis Negron, thank you for being a supportive friend and brother.

To my Irish brother, Brian O'Neill, a fellow Jersey boy from Secaucus, NJ: Thanks for advising me to sleep on your couch, drink all your wine, and eat your food when I moved to Hollywood to pursue my dreams. Brian, you gave me the mindset to take my acting career seriously when we were roommates in Weehawken, NJ. I'm also thankful for your help in getting my first SAG voucher as an extra on one of the films you were working on. I got to chill in Malibu for the first time and saw my childhood crush, Michelle Pfeiffer, on set. Thanks, dog! That gave me a path to join the union.

A big thank you To Lis Chirinos for giving me my first journal.

Shout out to my boy, Martin Cummins: Marty, you're my man! Thanks for always being a loyal friend. I always have a steak waiting for you.

To my homegirl, Anna Paris, my ride-or-die acting partner in the early Hollywood days: Thanks for driving my broke ass around to auditions when my car broke down on Laurel Canyon on my way to acting class. Love you!

To Juliana Dawson: Thank you for your guidance. Your expertise was paramount in my understanding of the end game of following through with this book.

To Sarah Belbita, thank you for your keen eye and thoughtful feedback.

Special thanks also go to Ewelina Lemanski for crafting the beautiful book cover design and Diana Perez-Alvarado for the cover photo and author photo.

A heartfelt thank you to my management team, Arthur Massei and Terrie Snell at Talent Ink NY-Chicago-LA, for consistently being genuine friends and guides.

To my agent, Barry Kolker, at the Carson Kolker Agency, thank you.

Thank you, Eileen O'Farrell, my first manager in Los Angeles. Eileen, you believed in me and guided me to my first big break, General Hospital. Gracias! Thank you, Enzo Lamblet—you were an integral part of my young career.

I am grateful for my West Coast representation and Ely Doryon from Coast-to-Coast Talent Group. To my first LA agent, Nikolas Rey, at The Alvarado Rey Agency.

A big shout-out to my Los Angeles crew. Your talents and support were vital in my acting journey: Juan Sola, Alejandro Cardenas, Tomiko Martinez, Pierre Derbier, Darlene Vazquetelles, Tom Parker, Vergi Rodriquez and Jeremy Luke. I learned so much just being around you all. Thank you for being my West Cost family.

ADRIAN ALVARADO

To Wayne Lopez: I met you when I first got to LA, and your advice to always bring it and always be prepared sticks with me to this day.

Thank you, Jonah Rooney, Veronica Collins Rooney, and Jessie Disla, for your friendship and support.

To Santiago "Santi" Gonzales: Thanks for bringing me into your circle when I first moved to Los Angeles and making me feel like I had the world as my oyster.

To all my Hudson County teachers: Great teachers are always awesome and true heroes. Ms. Maria Mateo, who cast me in the high school play when I was in third grade and later became my Spanish teacher in high school. Thank you, Ms. Mateo, for recognizing my talents and reminding me of them in high school. I'm forever grateful.

Mr. Charles Corcoran, the coolest English teacher ever. Thank you!

Mr. D'Angelo, for encouraging me in class to keep reading Shakespeare. Thank you.

A big Jersey City shout-out to my high school junior English teacher, Mrs. Linda Mahoney: Thank you for encouraging my pursuit of acting and making me aware of my bad diction.

Mr. Don Wonder, my first sensei and acting teacher: Thank you for sharing your knowledge. I'm always forever grateful. As a teacher, you went above and beyond to guide and give us all the realities and tools to prepare us to succeed. Thank you!

A shout-out to my university, NJCU. My professor, Anderson Johnson, and all my talented theater classmates—

Erzulie Mendoza, Megean Corcoran, Debra Sciancalepore, Brendan Wahlers, Roberto Cambeiro, and Roxana Arroyo: You all had an impact on my acting career and my college experience. Thanks to Lilli Marquez Markey, my first leading lady in our college production of Molière's Learned Ladies.

Thank you to the late, great Joe Palese, the best acting teacher I ever had. Joe had a way of talking to us actors that would generate raw natural reactions. He forced us to be ourselves in every scene. Thanks, Joe! Rest in peace.

A big thank you to General Hospital and casting director Mark Teschner, who kept bringing me in for callbacks because he saw something. You gave me my big break in television by casting me as Detective Cruz Rodriguez on General Hospital. Thanks, Mark. I'm grateful and humbled for the opportunity you gave me.

Thank you to Jill Pharren Phelps, who gave the green light for my character, Cruz Rodriguez, to come to Port Charles and give a little attitude. My experiences working on the show gave me invaluable lessons as a young professional performer.

I want to extend my deepest gratitude to Maurice Benard for blessing this memoir with his thoughtful blurb. Your words mean more to me than you know, and your support has added a layer of validation and encouragement that I will carry with me always. Thank you for being a guiding light and an inspiration, both in your work and in life.

ADRIAN ALVARADO

I want to honor all those who came before me, paved the way, gave me inspiration, and let me see myself in them. In their work. Legends past and present like the first Puerto Rican to win an Academy Award, José Ferrer. The Legend, Raul Julia. Actors I admire and look up to like Benicio Del Toro, Jennifer Lopez, Esai Morales, Jimmy Smits, and John Leguizamo.

I owe the inspiration for all my poetry to the original street pioneers of spoken word and the founders of the Nuyorican Poets Cafe—Miguel Piñero, Miguel Algarín, Pedro Pietri.

I would like to extend my deepest gratitude to Esmeralda Santiago, whose work has long been an inspiration to me. I was humbled when you graciously took the time to respond to my email and share your wisdom with me. Your storytelling advice resonated deeply, pushing me to dig deeper into my own narrative and honor the truth in every detail. Thank you for your encouragement, your insight, and for reminding me of the power and responsibility that comes with sharing our stories. Your words have left a lasting impact on my journey as a writer. I followed your advice and used my rage, love, fear and frustration to tell my story. Gracias.

Finally, to my beloved island, Puerto Rico. Te quiero, siempre. You are the pearl of the sea and the anchor of my spirit—always have been, always will be. I hope this story captures both the struggle and the beauty of our shared journey. Yo te quiero Puerto Rico!

References

discoverpuertorico.com. (n.d.). Retrieved from https://www.discoverpuertorico.com/article/everything-you-need-to-know-about-international-mojo-isleno-festival: https://www.discoverpuertorico.com

Library of Congress. (n.d.). Retrieved from Library of Congress, Research Guide: https://guides.loc.gov/latinx-civil-rights/jones-shafroth-act#:~:text=The%20Selective%20Service%20Act%20of,fought%20in%20World%20War%20II.

Living in Jersey City 1997-1998. (n.d.).

Minster, P. D. (2019, May 15). *https://www.thoughtco.com*. Retrieved from ThoughtCo.: https://www.thoughtco.com/biography-of-pedro-de-alvarado-2136555

Ortiz, J. D. (n.d.). Our Esquina.

Ruiz Torro, J. (n.d.). *https://library.brown.edu*. Retrieved from Brown University Library: https://library.brown.edu/create/modernlatinamerica/chapters/chapter-12-strategies-for-economic-developmen/puerto-ricos-operation-bootstrap/

Wikipedia. (n.d.). *https://en.wikipedia.org/*. Retrieved from Wikipedia: https://en.wikipedia.org/wiki/Aibonito,_Puerto_Rico

Wikipedia. (n.d.). *https://en.wikipedia.org/*. Retrieved from https://en.wikipedia.org/wiki/Skully_(game)

ADRIAN ALVARADO

www.ingramcontent.com/pod-product-compliance
Lightning Source LLC
Chambersburg PA
CBHW062048080426
42734CB00012B/2588